.invisible
invaders

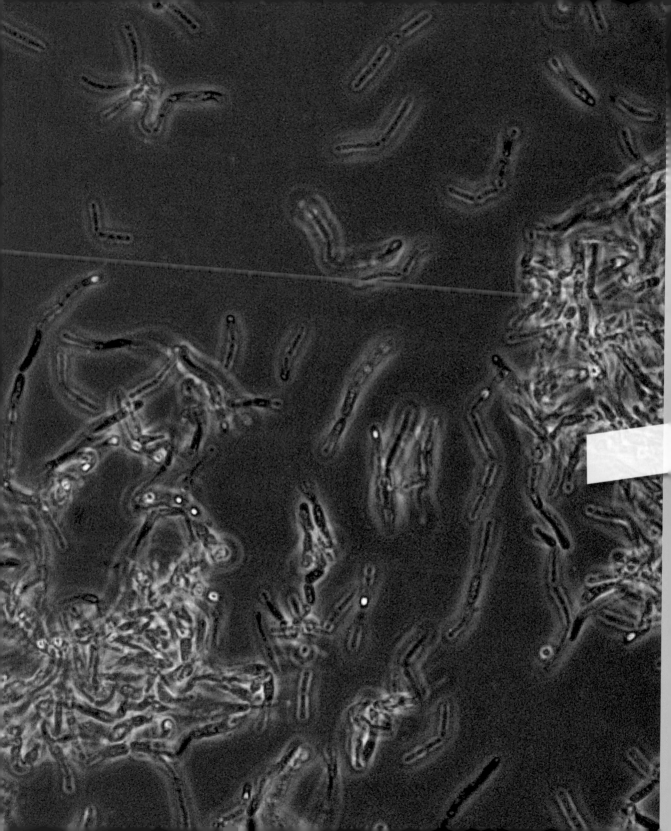

invisible invaders

DANGEROUS INFECTIOUS DISEASES

connie goldsmith

Twenty-First Century Books • Minneapolis

Special thanks to my writing partners, Erin Dealey, Patricia M. Newman, and Laura Torres, for their endless support and encouragement

Page two: A microscopic photograph of anthrax

Twenty-First Century Books
A division of Lerner Publishing Group
241 First Avenue North
Minneapolis, Minnesota 55401 U.S.A.

Website address: www.lernerbooks.com

Library of Congress Cataloging-in-Publication Data

Goldsmith, Connie, 1945–
    Invisible invaders : dangerous infectious diseases / by Connie Goldsmith.
      p.   cm. — (Discovery!)
    Includes bibliographical references and index.
    ISBN-13: 978–0–8225–3416–7 (lib. bdg. : alk. paper)
    ISBN-10: 0–8225–3416–9 (lib. bdg. : alk. paper)
    1. Emerging infectious diseases—Popular works. I. Title. II. Series: Discovery! (Minneapolis, Minn.)
    RA643.G66 2006
    362.196'9—dc22
                                               2005017271

Manufactured in the United States of America
1 2 3 4 5 6 – BP – 11 10 09 08 07 06

CONTENTS

INTRODUCTION
by Joseph Dalovisio, MD, past president of
The Infectious Diseases Society of America

You've probably heard a lot about infectious diseases lately. The headlines are full of reports about diseases such as avian influenza, West Nile virus, SARS, and anthrax. Even though these diseases are considered "news," infectious diseases have been around us from the beginning of time.

Infectious diseases are caused by microscopic organisms—including bacteria, viruses, fungi, and parasites—that penetrate the body's natural barriers and multiply to create symptoms that can range from mild to deadly. Although progress has been made in controlling or eradicating many infectious diseases, humankind remains vulnerable to a wide array of new and resurgent organisms. Infectious diseases have become a major concern worldwide in recent years as our environment has undergone rapid changes due to increased international travel, war, poverty, and other factors.

Infectious diseases can be as common as influenza (the flu) and pneumonia or as exotic as SARS or Ebola. Infectious diseases are the second-leading cause of death and the leading cause of disability worldwide. In the United States, infectious diseases are the third-leading cause of death. One of the deadliest infectious diseases is acquired immunodeficiency syndrome (AIDS), caused by the human immunodeficiency virus (HIV). According to the Centers for Disease Control and Prevention, approximately 3 million people die from HIV/AIDS each year. An estimated 42 million people are currently living with HIV/AIDS, and 14,000 new HIV infections occur daily worldwide.

Fortunately, there are many things you can do to protect against infectious diseases. Not having sex—or using condoms if you do—can prevent HIV infection. Other infectious diseases can be prevented by washing your hands, thoroughly cooking meats to avoid foodborne illnesses, and keeping up to date on immunizations. In fact, immunizations are one of the most effective ways to prevent serious infectious diseases. Between 50,000 and 70,000 adults and 300,000 children die each year from illnesses that can be prevented by vaccines. Public health measures that assure clean water supplies, adequate sewage treatment, and sanitary handling of food and milk also help control the spread of infectious diseases.

The fight against infectious diseases requires worldwide efforts by physicians, scientists, and public health officials. They gather information on diseases, report on outbreaks, and develop standards and guidelines for treating and controlling disease.

In terms of treatment, antibiotics and other disease-fighting drugs have played an important role in the fight against infectious diseases. Recently, however, some microorganisms have developed resistance to the drugs used against them. Modern physicians should prescribe antibiotics carefully. The more widely these drugs are used, the more likely it is that drug-resistant strains of diseases will emerge.

Infectious diseases can be an interesting and exciting field to learn about. Knowing where they come from, how they spread, and what to do if an outbreak occurs will help keep us all safe.

The Infectious Diseases Society of America is made up of physicians, health-care professionals, and scientists. Its purpose is to improve the health of individuals and society worldwide by promoting excellence in patient care and research related to infectious diseases.

CHAPTER 1

EMERGING INFECTIOUS DISEASES:
IT'S A SMALL WORLD AFTER ALL

A VILLAGE IN CHINA: Schools are closed, and shops and restaurants are deserted. A few masked people scurry through the silent streets, stumbling to keep out of one another's way. A man streaks by on a bicycle, feet pumping like crazy, desperate to reach the safety of home. A bulging backpack dangles behind him. The man anxiously scans the street as he stops for a second to tighten the mask covering his mouth and nose. He shouldn't even be out because his family is under quarantine. But his children needed vegetables and rice, and the only open market was miles away. If he's lucky, the police won't catch him.

Does this scene sound like something out of a history book? Police-enforced quarantine? Protective face masks? In fact, this is what a street in China looked like in 2003 when the first new infectious disease of the twenty-first century appeared. Throughout Southeast Asia, public places were closed and hundreds of thousands of people were quarantined at home or in hospitals. By the time health officials recognized the existence of this new disease, air travelers had already spread it around the world. In just weeks, it reached thirty countries, made

Commuters in Hong Kong wear face masks to protect themselves against severe acute respiratory syndrome (SARS) in April 2003.

thousands of people sick, and killed hundreds of them. The disease was named severe acute respiratory syndrome (SARS).

One hundred years ago, children everywhere routinely died of diseases such as measles and diphtheria. Pneumonia and flu killed millions. Small cuts became savage infections. Battlefield wounds were deadly to soldiers on all sides. Strep throat could result in heart damage. Polio crippled hundreds of thousands of U.S. children. But doctors and scientists fought back, introducing improved sanitation and better personal hygiene. They also developed vaccines to prevent diseases, and antibiotics to cure them.

In 1967 U.S. surgeon general William H. Stewart declared victory over infectious diseases. He suggested the nation turn its attention to the more important threat of chronic illnesses—those that last a long time or progress slowly and are not caused by infection or passed by contact. Public health agencies lost funding as research efforts were redirected toward discovering the causes of heart disease and cancer. Those illnesses became the new frontier of medicine.

But we badly underestimated the power of infectious diseases. After decades of decline, deaths from infectious diseases in the United States increased by nearly 60 percent between 1980 and 2000. Currently, half the deaths in developing countries are caused by infectious diseases. Each hour infections kill about 1,500 people worldwide, half of them children under five years old. The reemergence of old diseases caught health officials off guard. And the world was poorly prepared for the emergence of new infectious diseases—especially AIDS.

More than thirty-five new infectious diseases have come to light since the early 1970s. Emerging diseases, such as SARS, are those that have never before been found in humans or those that may have infected humans but went unrecognized, such as hantavirus. Reemerging diseases, including tuberculosis and yellow fever, were previously under control but have now strengthened or spread to new regions. Some diseases were entrenched in other countries but have only recently appeared in the United States, such as West Nile virus.

All infectious diseases are caused by microbes. These tiny organisms—too small to be seen by the naked eye—live everywhere on Earth. They include bacteria, viruses, fungi, and parasites. Many microbes do not cause any disease or illness. Those that make people or animals sick are called pathogens. Scientists estimate that less than 1 percent of the world's microbes have been identified, so it's likely that humans will be affected by many other new pathogens in the future.

why now?

No simple explanation exists for the emergence of so many new infectious diseases. Scientists believe it's due to the complex interactions between humans and their environment. In 2003 the Institute of Medicine published a report called "Microbial Threats to Health: Emergence, Detection, and Response." It describes how our living conditions have contributed to the rise of new and reemerging infectious diseases. These conditions include:

Turning up the Heat: Many people worry about global warming—a gradual increase in Earth's average temperature partially caused by human activities such as the burning of fossil fuels (coal, oil, and natural gas). These fuels release substances into the atmosphere that allow heat to be trapped. Scientists who study the weather believe Earth's temperature could rise between 2.5°F and 10.4°F (1.4–5.8°C) by the year 2100.

As a result of this warming, animals and insects that prefer warmer temperatures would move into areas that are currently too cold for them. Diseases carried by tropical mosquitoes, such as malaria, yellow fever, and dengue fever, could become commonplace in North America. If temperatures continue to climb, more than half the world's people could be at risk for contracting malaria.

Even natural climate changes can lead to an outbreak of infectious disease. El Niño, a warming of the ocean waters off South America, occurs every three to seven years. These warm waters change weather patterns around the world for months, resulting in increased rainfall in some areas and droughts in other areas. Scientists believe that unusually heavy rainfall caused by El Niño in 1993 resulted in an outbreak of hantavirus in the southwestern United States.

Dangerous Critters: About 75 percent of emerging infections are transmitted from animals to humans. Changing weather patterns aren't the only reason that animal-to-human transmission of diseases may increase. Anything that creates closer contact between animals and humans can put humans at risk. For example, black-legged ticks carry Lyme disease. When builders put up new housing developments in wooded areas, people are more likely to come into contact with those ticks.

In Africa logging companies regularly set up camps in remote forests. The camps are far away from food supplies, so the workers often hunt wild animals for food. Imagine that one day a man cuts his finger while on the job. That night he kills a monkey and butchers it for dinner. The man's open cut could easily come in contact with the monkey's blood. Such contact between humans and infected monkeys probably led to the world's very first cases of HIV.

Crowded Conditions: The world's population is continually growing. In 1900 about 1.5 billion people were alive. By 2000 the number had increased to 6 billion. Across the globe, many people are flocking to big cities. In 1975 only five cities had 10 million or more people. By 2000 nineteen cities had populations that large. When people live in very close contact in these huge cities, they can readily catch infectious diseases from one another. For example, tuberculosis, a disease spread through the air, can easily spread among people who live crammed together in crowded, shoddy housing.

Poverty and War: War causes people around the world to flee their homes and move into refugee camps. There, people are often forced into crowded, unsanitary conditions. Refugees

A mother holds her sick, malnourished child in a refugee camp in the central African country of Chad.

may not have access to clean drinking water, so cholera or other diseases may spread quickly through the camps. Away from their homes, refugees cannot grow crops and must often rely on aid organizations for food. Without enough food, people quickly become malnourished and more susceptible to disease. The camps are likely to have too few health care workers and inadequate medical supplies to help all the sick and injured. In addition, soldiers living and fighting in close quarters can easily spread disease. Three out of four deaths during and after a war are due to illness and starvation, not the conflict itself.

Neglecting the Basics: Public health agencies are racing to catch up with neglected activities such as disease surveillance and health education. If health officials don't know when an outbreak of a disease is taking place, they can't figure out how to slow it down or stop it. If they don't teach the basics of disease prevention, illness spreads faster. Testing the water supply to ensure it's free of pathogens is crucial, but some countries don't have the money to do this. A number of nations don't adequately vaccinate children against preventable diseases such as measles and polio. In hospitals health-care workers who don't follow proper procedures can cause hospital-acquired infections. People who enter the hospital for simple operations or mild illnesses may end up with life-threatening infections.

Risky Behaviors: High-risk behaviors such as unprotected sexual activity spreads sexually transmitted diseases such as AIDS, gonorrhea, and genital herpes. Intravenous drug use can spread illnesses such as AIDS and hepatitis C, because drug addicts often share dirty needles. Many of the four million Americans with hepatitis C got it from injecting illegal drugs. In addition, many illegal drugs can impair decision making, which can lead users to engage in other risky behaviors.

Fast as a Speeding Plane: Millions of people, animals, and crates of food travel around the world daily, greatly speeding the rate at which infections spread. In 2000 more than one billion people traveled by plane. Billions more traveled by ship, train, bus, or automobile. In the nineteenth century, it took one year to circle the globe by ship. In the twenty-first century, a person can travel around the world by plane in less than 36 hours! Because of air travel, SARS reached 30 countries in just a few weeks in 2003. Travelers infected others around them before they even realized they were sick.

Air travel allows people to travel quickly from one country to another, but it can also spread disease around the world.

Mammals, birds, fish, and reptiles are all brought from one country to another to be sold as pets. Human monkeypox reached the United States in 2003 when imported African rodents infected American prairie dogs that were sold as pets. Our food comes from many countries as well. Fruit and vegetables arrive daily from Mexico, Central America, and South America to supply our demand for fresh produce year-round. Imported raspberries and lettuce grown in fields irrigated with contaminated water caused a dozen outbreaks of parasitic diseases in the past decade.

High-Tech Problems: Advances in medical technology have opened new ways to transfer infectious organisms from one person to another. Each year in the United States, about 23 million units of blood and blood products are transfused into people because of injuries, surgical procedures, and certain medical conditions. Blood transfusions save many lives, but some organisms, such as those that cause AIDS, hepatitis C, malaria, and West Nile virus can be transmitted by infected blood. Blood is always tested for these diseases as well as many others, but tests don't exist for all diseases. Despite our precautions, people occasionally get sick from blood transfusions.

Modern medicine has also given us the miracle of lifesaving organ transplants. About 23,000 organ transplants and over half a million tissue transplants (such as cartilage and bone) are performed each year. Like blood, organs and tissues are carefully screened for infectious organisms before being given to patients. Still, occasionally an organ donor has an unrecognized infection that is transmitted to the organ recipient. In a few cases, several people have gotten ill or died after receiving organs and tissues from one infected person.

We have a serious shortage of organs for transplant. Each year only about one-third of the people who need organ transplants get them. Researchers are looking into xenotransplantation—the transplanting of animal organs or tissues into humans. For example, valves from pig hearts were successfully transplanted into human hearts before artificial heart valves were developed. While animal organs may offer a chance for life to people desperately needing organs, scientists are concerned that such organs could carry unrecognized animal diseases into humans.

New farming techniques that make it possible to raise a large number of animals in a confined space have led to other health problems. Most food animals are raised not on family farms but on "factory" farms. For example, fifty thousand chickens may live in a warehouselike building where cages are stacked one over the other. Chicken droppings fall into the cages below, contaminating food and water. Beef cattle are crowded together in tiny

Diseases spread quickly when farmers keep animals in cramped quarters.

pens while they are fattened up for slaughter. These high concentrations of animals result in huge amounts of manure in small areas. Animals, just like humans, have a lot of bacteria in their feces. In these farming factories, animals not only make one another sick more often, the massive quantity of manure can seep into our water and food supplies and make us sick.

Imperfect Immune Systems: Human beings have lived with certain types of pathogens, such as cold viruses, for thousands of years. We're very good at fighting these pathogens off before they make us seriously ill. But when humans are exposed to a brand-new infectious agent, our immune systems can't fight it off so quickly. That's one reason why new diseases can be so deadly, even for people with healthy immune systems. And not everyone has an immune system that's in perfect condition. Very young children, pregnant women, malnourished people, and older adults often have more trouble fighting off infections. Even with an adequate diet and good medical care, these people are especially vulnerable to disease.

Certain medical conditions can also impair the immune system. People with AIDS are much more susceptible to infections than other people. Tuberculosis is the most common cause of death among AIDS patients. Cancer patients receiving chemotherapy or radiation treatments are also at high risk for infections. People who receive organ transplants must take special drugs that suppress their immune systems to keep their body from rejecting the transplant. These medications put organ recipients at risk for infectious diseases.

Mutating Microbes: Microbes often undergo changes called mutations. Some mutations make them more dangerous to humans. Over time some types of microbes become able to bypass the human immune system. Others become resistant to drugs,

KNOW YOUR 'DEMICS

As diseases make their way around the world, different terms are used to describe how widespread they are. An outbreak occurs when a disease hits a few people in a localized region. So far, Ebola has been limited to outbreaks in a handful of African villages. When a disease is constantly present in a particular location, it's considered endemic. Dengue fever is endemic to much of South America. An epidemic occurs when a disease strikes many people in several regions at the same time. West Nile virus can be called an epidemic as it spreads across North America. A pandemic affects many people in many parts of the world at the same time. The world experienced two pandemics in the twentieth century—the Spanish flu of 1918–1919 and HIV/AIDS, first identified in the early 1980s.

such as antibiotics, that are used to kill them. This can happen when people don't take their antibiotics exactly as prescribed by their doctor. Some people stop taking the antibiotics when they feel better. Then, only the weakest bacteria have been killed. The stronger bacteria that resisted antibiotics remain alive to multiply and spread.

Sometimes two different microbes meet and swap some of their genetic material. The resulting microbes may have new traits that make them especially harmful. One strain of the common bacterium *E. coli* contains genetic material from a group of bacteria called *Shigella,* which cause severe diarrhea. This particular kind of *E. coli*—an emerging strain called *E. coli O157:H7*—makes people much sicker than other types do.

Not by Accident: Humans are vulnerable to bioterrorism, the use of deadly germs to kill or terrorize an enemy. Health authorities especially fear anthrax, plague, and smallpox as weapons. In 2001 anthrax spores were mailed to several U.S. cities, resulting in five deaths. Scientists and government officials fear that a future attack could be much deadlier. Preventing or responding to a bioterrorist attack is immensely complicated and requires a lot of advance planning. It involves police and other security forces just as much as it involves health-care workers.

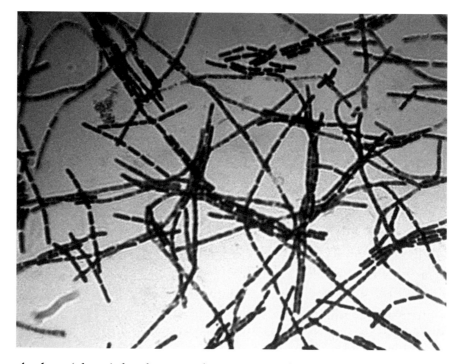

Anthrax (above) *has been used as a weapon by terrorists.*

who's WHO?

We need to plan for future outbreaks and work to prevent the spread of existing diseases. And when an outbreak hits, people need an organized way to respond. Doctors and scientists must figure out what's causing the disease, how it's transmitted, how fast it's spreading, and what steps should be taken to stop it. And they need to do all of this very quickly! When a previously unknown infectious agent causes an outbreak, getting the answers to these questions can be especially difficult.

Three major organizations carry out many of the activities that protect and promote world health. All of them maintain excellent, up-to-date websites about emerging and reemerging infectious diseases, including comprehensive information about how to prevent and treat them.

Part of the United Nations, the World Health Organization (WHO) is governed by the 192 countries making up the World Health Assembly. The agency's main objective is to promote the highest possible level of health for people everywhere. Among its many tasks, WHO negotiates and maintains national and global partnerships related to world health activities. WHO is headquartered in Geneva, Switzerland. Its regional office for North and South America is in Washington, D.C.

The Centers for Disease Control and Prevention (CDC) is an agency of the U.S. Department of Health and Human Services. It tracks and monitors infectious diseases and sends teams to investigate epidemics and outbreaks worldwide. It's the leading federal agency charged with protecting the health and safety of Americans at home and abroad. The CDC is headquartered in Atlanta, Georgia.

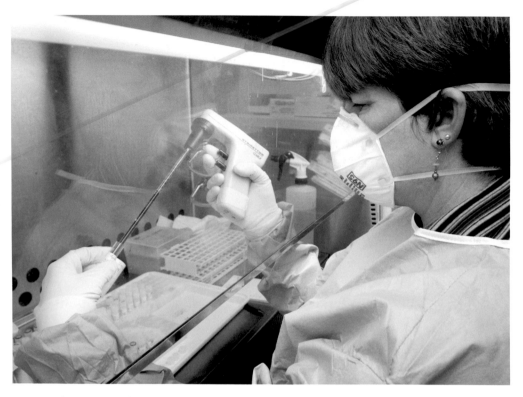

A scientist from the CDC (above) *studies the SARS virus.*

The National Institute of Allergy and Infectious Diseases (NIAID) is one of the National Institutes of Health. It conducts and funds basic research into preventing, diagnosing, and treating infectious diseases. Some of its special projects include mapping the genetic makeup of microbes, researching malaria and influenza, and developing vaccines for HIV and other infectious diseases. NIAID is based in Bethesda, Maryland.

According to Dr. Anthony S. Fauci, director of NIAID, "The twenty-first century will see an ever-increasing emphasis on infectious diseases, both because of the certainty that emerging and re-emerging diseases will continue to challenge us, and because globalization has led to an increased awareness of and commitment to addressing the terrible burden of infectious diseases in developing nations."

The nations and people of the world are truly globalized—interconnected through trade, travel, and popular culture. A town in China quarantined because of SARS, a remote village in Angola decimated by Marburg, neighborhoods in New York and Los Angeles hit by AIDS—in this world, in this time, an outbreak of infectious disease anywhere threatens the health of people everywhere.

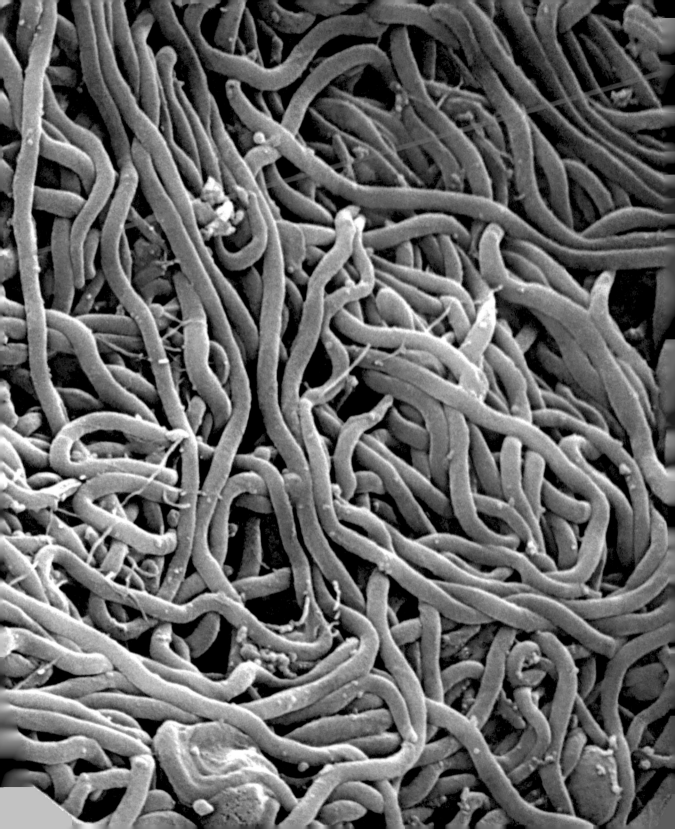

CHAPTER 2

BACTERIAL DISEASES:
STILL GOING STRONG AFTER THREE BILLION YEARS

We eat bacteria in sandwiches and ice cream, on peaches and tomatoes. We drink them with water and lemonade. And we suck them into our mouths and noses every time we breathe. Some get to us by way of flea or mosquito bites, and others reach us when we touch an animal at a petting zoo. Bacteria live on our skin and inside our bodies. Our bodies contain ten times as many bacteria as human cells. We pass them on to other people by sneezing, coughing, shaking hands, and kissing.

Bacteria are single-celled organisms. They are neither plants nor animals. Scientists place them in their own category, the kingdom Prokaryotae. Most bacteria can be seen with a good microscope. Scientists classify them based on their shapes: spherical (coccus), rodlike (bacillus), or curved or spiral-shaped (spirillum or spirochete). Some bacteria have flagella—tail-like projections—that propel them around. Others travel with the flow of fluids. A sturdy cell wall surrounds most bacteria and a tangled clump of genetic material lies inside.

Bacteria may be the most ancient life-forms on Earth. Their imprints have been found in fossils estimated to be more than three billion years old. Bacteria can live just about anywhere. Different types of bacteria live in freezing-cold arctic ice, in boiling-hot springs, and even in the acid that bubbles inside human stomachs. They cover Earth's face, and a good many

Borrelia burgdorferi *is an example of a spirochete bacteria.*

more live in Earth's interior. So many kinds of bacteria exist that scientists believe we've discovered only 1 percent of them.

All bacteria require nutrients, and most require oxygen. Bacteria reproduce by growing until they are double in size, then they simply split in half. They are very fertile: some species can crank out a new generation every 30 minutes. Under harsh conditions, some kinds of bacteria form hard shells and become spores. The spores remain alive but inactive until conditions are once again favorable.

A BACTERIUM
(cross section)

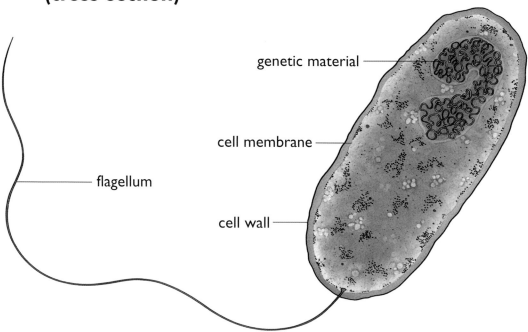

genetic material

cell membrane

flagellum

cell wall

While most bacteria aren't dangerous to people and some are quite useful, others can cause disease. Inside the human body, some harmful bacteria cause damage by releasing chemical poisons called toxins. Toxins kill human cells, producing symptoms of illness. Other bacteria grow so fast that they crowd out healthy cells.

Our immune system overpowers many pathogenic bacteria, but medication is needed to treat others. Many bacterial diseases are treated by medicines called antibiotics. The best-known antibiotic is penicillin. Some bacterial diseases, such as diphtheria, tetanus, and whooping cough, can be prevented by vaccination.

escherichia coli O157:H7

"My tummy hurts, Mama," Anna wailed. Three-year-old Anna had been having stomachaches and diarrhea for days. Her doctor couldn't figure out what was making her sick. Finally, Anna's mother took her to the hospital. There, doctors realized that Anna's kidneys were failing. She'd been infected with E. coli O157:H7 *by drinking unpasteurized apple juice. Anna was lucky. Even though she was sick for months, she finally recovered. Seventy other children got sick from drinking the same apple juice, and one died.*

The bacterium *E. coli O157:H7* first gained notice when it showed up in hamburgers sold by two major fast-food restaurants. In 1982 an outbreak occurred in undercooked burgers sold by McDonald's. During the next few years twenty-two smaller outbreaks happened, but they didn't receive much attention. The worst outbreak occurred in 1993 at Jack-in-the-Box

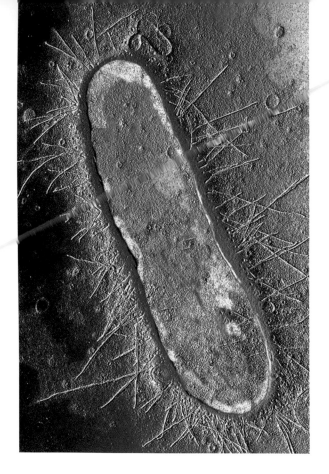

E. coli normally inhabits the human intestine. Under certain conditions, this bacterium can cause infection.

restaurants. After eating undercooked burgers, more than seven hundred people got sick and four children died.

Hundreds of strains of *E. coli* normally live in our bodies. Most of them don't cause any trouble. But scientists have found an important difference in the genetic material of *E. coli O157:H7*. All bacteria carry their genetic information in their deoxyribonucleic acid (DNA). DNA has all the information the bacteria need to live and grow. The DNA contains genes that tell the bacteria what to do and how to do it. Somehow, *E. coli O157:H7* picked up a gene from *Shigella* bacteria. This particular gene instructs the bacterium to make a substance known as a Shiga toxin.

E. coli O157:H7 bacteria can contaminate food in several ways. They live in the intestines of about half of all cattle. When a cow is slaughtered, bacteria may travel out of the intestines and into parts of the cow that are used for food.

Ground beef is the most common source of infection because grinding disperses bacteria throughout the meat. In hamburger-making plants, meat from many, many animals is mixed together. Tainted meat from a single animal can spread *E. coli O157:H7* to 8 tons (7 metric tons) of ground beef. Cooking beef kills the bacteria, but only if the meat is heated to at least 160°F (71°C).

E. coli O157:H7 is also present in cattle manure. Farmers frequently use the manure to fertilize fields and orchards. In Anna's case, perhaps a few apples dropped off a tree, rolled into manure that had been spread on the ground below, and picked up some *E. coli*. When the apples were squeezed and bottled, the juice was not pasteurized. Pasteurization is the heating of milk, juice, or other liquids to kill any microorganisms that are present. Unpasteurized beverages may contain dangerous bacteria. Anna drank live *E. coli O157:H7* in her juice.

Over the past few years, petting zoos have been identified as an important source of *E. coli O157:H7* infection in young children.

Pasteurized beverages have been heated to ensure they are free of dangerous bacteria.

Dozens of children and several adults were infected by the bacterium in 2004 and 2005 after touching animals at petting zoos in North Carolina and Florida. Touching the animal spreads bacteria to the hands, and bacteria enter the body when people touch their mouth or their food.

When a person eats or drinks something containing *E. coli O157:H7,* the bacteria travel to the intestines and release the Shiga toxin, causing severe abdominal pain. The bacteria damage the cells lining the intestines. The ruined cells pass from the body as bloody diarrhea. Once the protective intestinal lining has been destroyed, the bacteria can enter the blood system and attack other body systems.

As the toxin circulates through the body, it damages red blood cells and the kidneys. *E. coli O157:H7* is the most common cause of sudden kidney failure in U.S. children. The very sickest people need blood transfusions and dialysis, a process for cleaning the blood when the kidneys fail. Some children require kidney transplants. Survivors can be left with seizures, blindness, or paralysis caused by bleeding into the brain. In the United States, *E. coli O157:H7* sickens about 73,000 people each year and kills about 60. For every confirmed case, probably a dozen or more aren't reported.

Medications will not cure patients infected with *E. coli O157:H7.* Antibiotics that work for many bacterial infections don't work against this strain of *E. coli.* Scientists believe the bacterium is resistant to antibiotics because for many years farmers have been giving cattle and other livestock antibiotics to help them grow. Over time, the antibiotics kill all the weaker strains of *E. coli.* Only the strongest bacteria—those not affected by antibiotics—remain. These bacteria divide and produce more antibiotic-resistant bacteria. When humans become infected with these bacteria, nothing can be done except wait for the body's natural defenses to fight them. Fortunately, most people recover from *E. coli O157:H7* infections on their own.

We can help prevent infection by thoroughly cooking beef, drinking only pasteurized beverages, and washing all fruits and vegetables. Wash your hands with soap and hot water after touching animals, either your own pets or petting zoo animals. Wash your hands after going to the bathroom and before preparing food to avoid transferring any bacteria from your hands to other surfaces, which could pass the illness along to someone else.

lyme disease

"I was seventeen years old when I got Lyme disease," says Katie. She had nausea, swollen glands, and an itchy rash on her feet. "My knees hurt so much that I had to drop out of my swim meet." Katie went to see her doctor, and she tested positive for Lyme disease. She took oral and intravenous antibiotics off and on for several years for her swollen, painful joints. Katie is still sick. "I can only go to school part-time. Every day, I search for some new treatment that will get me healthy."

Usually doctors are the ones who first notice a new disease. But two mothers were the first people to call attention to Lyme disease (LD). In 1975 a worried mother in Lyme, Connecticut, took her children from doctor to doctor. They had rashes and swollen, painful joints. Doctors were baffled. A month later, another mother called the Connecticut Health Department to report an outbreak of what seemed like rheumatoid arthritis among children in her neighborhood. That disease causes swollen, painful joints and is uncommon in young children.

Soon doctors had found bad cases of arthritis in 39 children and 12 adults in Lyme. Some people remembered having a circular rash before the joint pains began. That gave the doctors a clue. They knew that tick bites could cause similar rashes. Doctors believed that ticks in the region were carrying a new disease. They named it Lyme disease.

At the time, scientists believed that all the bacteria in the world had been discovered, so they thought a virus caused LD. But no matter how hard researchers looked for a virus, it just wasn't there. Finally a U.S. scientist identified a bacterium as the cause. In 1982 the bacterium was named *Borrelia burgdorferi* after Willy Burgdorfer, the doctor who found it.

Black-legged ticks (also known as deer ticks) carry the bacteria in their gut. The tick has a two-year life cycle and bites deer, mice, and humans. Black-legged ticks are tiny. Adult black-legged ticks are .08 to .16 inches (2 to 4 mm). Nymphs—immature ticks—look like grains of pepper.

Tiny black-legged ticks (left) *are the vectors, or carriers, of Lyme disease. An early sign of the disease is a bull's eye rash* (right).

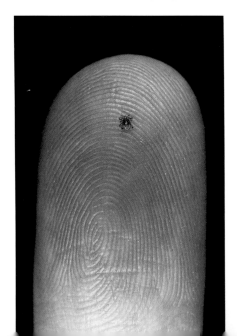 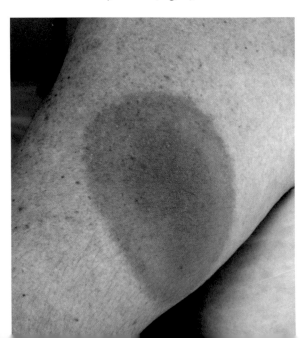

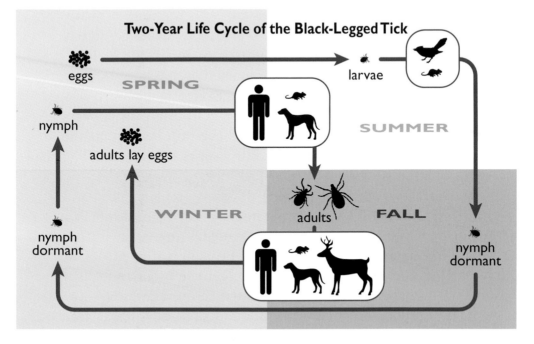

Two-Year Life Cycle of the Black-Legged Tick

eggs

SPRING

larvae

nymph

SUMMER

adults lay eggs

WINTER

adults

FALL

nymph
dormant

nymph
dormant

People get LD when a black-legged tick bites them. Ticks won't jump onto you or drop out of trees into your hair. Instead, ticks lurk on bushes and tall grass, waiting for you or another animal to brush against them. Once on your body, they move toward hairy places—the groin, armpit, or scalp. Ticks feed by inserting their mouthparts through the skin. It takes several days for a tick to fill up with blood. As an infected tick feeds, LD bacteria enter the bloodstream. Adult ticks are often found and removed before they've finished feeding. But nymphs are so small that they're easily overlooked. The longer an infected tick remains on your body, the greater the chance it will infect you with LD.

About 95 percent of LD cases occur in Connecticut, Delaware, Maine, Maryland, Massachusetts, Minnesota, New Jersey, New Hampshire, New York, Pennsylvania, Rhode Island,

and Wisconsin, although the disease has been found in nearly every state. Between 1990 and 2002, LD sickened nearly 200,000 Americans, about 24,000 of them in 2002 alone. Thousands more cases may go unreported each year.

After infection, it can take anywhere from a few days to several months for symptoms to develop. Often a rash appears where the tick was. It's called a bull's-eye rash because at the center is a white circle, surrounded by a series of red rings. The rash can last a few days or many weeks.

As time goes on, infected people usually feel very tired and have headaches and fever. Lymph nodes in the neck, armpit, or groin may swell. LD can spread to nearly any organ in the body. About four out of ten infected people suffer problems with their nervous system. LD can infect the brain and spinal cord or damage nerves that control the senses and facial muscles. It may weaken muscles throughout the body. Knees may swell painfully, making sufferers limp. Less often, LD damages the liver, kidneys, or heart. It can even cause psychiatric symptoms such as depression and panic attacks. Some people fight the symptoms of LD for years.

It can be hard to diagnose LD, especially if the bull's-eye rash isn't present. Blood tests may be negative if done too early after infection. The tests check for the presence of antibodies, substances formed in the blood to help fight off invading organisms. Several weeks may pass, however, before an infected person develops antibodies. None of the tests for LD is foolproof because the bacteria can hide in the immune system, making them impossible to detect. Several antibiotics can help LD sufferers, especially if given early. People with severe cases need intravenous medications for weeks or months. Occasionally a patient may not respond to any treatment.

It's best to avoid getting LD in the first place by avoiding tick bites. Wear long-sleeved shirts and long pants when walking in areas where ticks live. Wear a hat and tie back long hair. Use an insect repellent containing the chemical DEET to discourage ticks. Be sure to thoroughly check your hair and body for ticks every day. If you find a tick, ask your doctor if you should be tested for LD.

In 1998 a vaccine to help prevent LD became available. However, the vaccine was inconvenient because three injections over a year were required for full effectiveness. While it reduced a person's risk of developing LD, it didn't provide guaranteed protection. Some people also experienced side effects. In 2002 the company that produced the vaccine pulled it off the market saying there wasn't enough demand for it.

Scientists continue to study LD. Specific NIAID research includes learning more about how ticks carry and spread LD, trying to develop a new vaccine, improving antibiotic treatment, developing more accurate tests to diagnose LD, and trying to understand more clearly how the bacterium affects the human immune system.

tuberculosis

"My son was recently diagnosed with active TB," said the mother of a teenage boy. The doctors never found out how he got sick. He wasn't the typical TB patient—he wasn't homeless, an alcoholic, or a drug user. He wasn't HIV positive or malnourished, and he'd never been out of the country. Even though the boy had most of the common symptoms of TB, five doctors missed the diagnosis. Finally, a lung specialist discovered the TB. His mother warned, "People need to be trained to catch and stop TB."

The three infectious diseases that kill the most people world-wide are TB, HIV/AIDS, and malaria. TB has been killing people for thousands of years. The bones of cave dwellers and the spines of Egyptian mummies show signs of TB infection. It was the most widespread disease of ancient Greece, where it was usually fatal. The Greek physician Hippocrates was the first to accurately describe TB. He named it phthisis after the Greek word for "consumption," because TB seemed to eat up the body of its victims.

The number of TB cases plummeted in the middle of the twentieth century after antibiotics came into wide use. But the world was in for a nasty surprise. Around 1985 TB resurfaced as a major cause of infectious disease around the world. Why? Health officials had become complacent about TB's dangers. Medical and financial resources had been directed toward studying other illnesses such as AIDS, cancer, and heart disease.

TB is caused by the bacterium *Mycobacterium tuberculosis.* This bacterium is known for being slow—very slow. While most bacteria double in number every twenty to thirty minutes, *M. tuberculosis* takes twenty-four hours to double. TB is passed through the air by coughing, talking, or sneezing, but it isn't as contagious as a cold or the flu. Once inhaled, the bacteria travel down the throat and into the lungs. Even then most people with normal immune systems won't get sick.

TB kills about 2 million people each year, most of them in developing countries. According to WHO, one-third of the world's population is infected with TB. Every second, a new person becomes infected. When large numbers of people crowd together in poverty, infectious diseases flourish. When refugees surge back and forth across national borders, TB goes along for the ride.

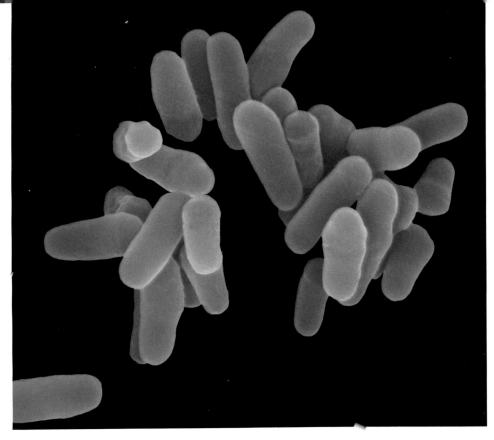

Rod-shaped mycobacterium tuberculosis *cause TB.*

While anyone can get TB, certain groups of people are more likely to get it. People in developing countries are more likely to have TB and may bring it with them when they immigrate to the United States. Other people at high risk for TB are those living in close contact with someone who has it, people livi in crowded conditions such as prisons, and malnourished pe ple such as alcoholics and drug users. In the United States, T is more common in African Americans than Caucasians, and it on the rise among Hispanics, Asians, and Pacific Islanders. Th disease is especially dangerous for people with compromisec immune systems. TB is the leading cause of death for HIV-infected people.

ATTACK OF THE SUPERBUGS

Back when your grandparents were children, infectious diseases were extremely dangerous. A child could die of tetanus. A ruptured appendix could kill a teen. Young mothers died of childbirth infections. Battlefield wounds routinely killed soldiers. Older people often died from pneumonia. Then came the miracle drugs called antibiotics. They've saved millions of lives since they came into widespread use in 1945. After that, many people thought infectious diseases would become a thing of the past.

But we celebrated too soon. Humans underestimated bacteria's ability to fight back against the antibiotics intended to destroy them. Bacteria are incredibly adaptable. Not only do most of them reproduce extremely fast, they also take in new genetic material from other organisms, which may mutate to increase their ability to resist antibiotics.

Since the 1980s, deaths from bacterial infections have climbed nearly 60 percent. Some bacteria are resistant to many, if not all, of the antibiotics that used to promptly kill them. Many doctors believe that the increase in antibiotic-resistant bacterial infections is a bigger danger to the world than bioterrorism. They fear that in the future, common infections might become as untreatable as they were before antibiotics were discovered.

This threat has been largely brought on because of the improper use of antibiotics. Nearly half of all prescriptions for antibiotics are unnecessary. They don't work against viruses, such as the ones that cause colds and the flu. Yet people sometimes demand antibiotics when they're sick with these diseases, and harried doctors may give patients prescriptions "just in case" their illness is bacterial.

Antibiotics given to animals cause just as many problems as those given to humans do. Millions of pounds of antibiotics are added to animal and poultry food every year. This food is fed to healthy animals to help them grow a little bit bigger and faster. Bacteria living inside the animals gradually grow resistant to the antibiotics. Waste

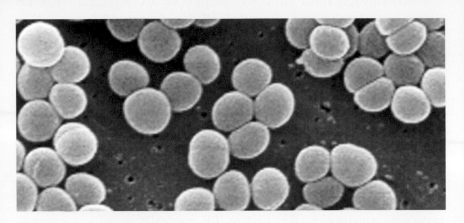

Some types of Staphylococcus aureus *have become resistant to antibiotics.*

products containing antibiotic-resistant bacteria seep into rivers and streams, spreading them throughout the environment.

Each year about 200,000 people get infections while they're in the hospital, and 90,000 of them die from their infections. Perhaps the most dangerous infection is caused by the *Staphylococcus aureus,* or staph, bacterium. Approximately one-third of people carry these bacteria in their nose or on their skin, and sometimes they cause an infection. One type of staph resists the strongest form of penicillin—methicillin—and it has been nicknamed MRSA, for methicillin-resistant *Staphylococcus aureus.* MRSA infections resist most antibiotics. Some cannot be cured at all. MRSA infections have also spread to the community. High school and college athletes may spread MRSA infections by sharing towels and sports equipment. MRSA infections have spread through professional football teams when they shared hot tubs.

Be smart about antibiotics. Don't demand them from your doctor. If you do get a prescription for antibiotics, take them exactly as prescribed. Don't stop taking them when you feel better. Never share antibiotics with other people or take any of theirs. Everyone can help to stop the spread of antibiotic-resistant bacterial infections.

Even though huge numbers of people are infected with TB bacteria, only about one in ten will develop the disease. It can lie dormant in the body for years or even a lifetime. People who carry TB bacteria but aren't sick are said to have a latent, or dormant, infection. They are not contagious. People who are sick with TB have a bad cough and chest pain. They may bring up bloody sputum when they cough. They will have a fever and night sweats and may lose weight because they don't have much of an appetite.

When a doctor suspects someone has TB, several tests may be performed. If a person tests positive for TB, the doctor will prescribe antibiotics. But just as TB bacteria are slow to reproduce and to infect, they are also slow to die. People must take their medications for six to nine months to completely eliminate the bacteria.

Why do so many people die of TB if it can be cured? Some people can't afford medication. People being treated for it often start feeling better after a few weeks and stop taking their medications. But then the bacteria most resistant to the antibiotics are still alive. These resistant bacteria continue reproducing and later make the person even sicker. Also, only about nine out of ten cases can be cured with a combination of medications. Some strains of TB have become resistant to most, if not all, antibiotics. The increase in antibiotic-resistant TB is one reason why it's been labeled as a reemerging disease. Only half of the people with the most drug-resistant strain of TB can be cured.

In many parts of the world, the TB vaccine BCG is given to newborns. BCG doesn't prevent TB infection, but it can prevent TB disease. The vaccine is made of live bacteria, which makes it dangerous for HIV-infected people. The period of protection varies, and people vaccinated with BCG will always have positive TB tests, so doctors have trouble determining whether or not a BCG-vaccinated person has TB disease. As a result, the vaccine is seldom used in the United States. The NIAID is funding research into a number of new vaccines for TB, but none is expected to be available for several years.

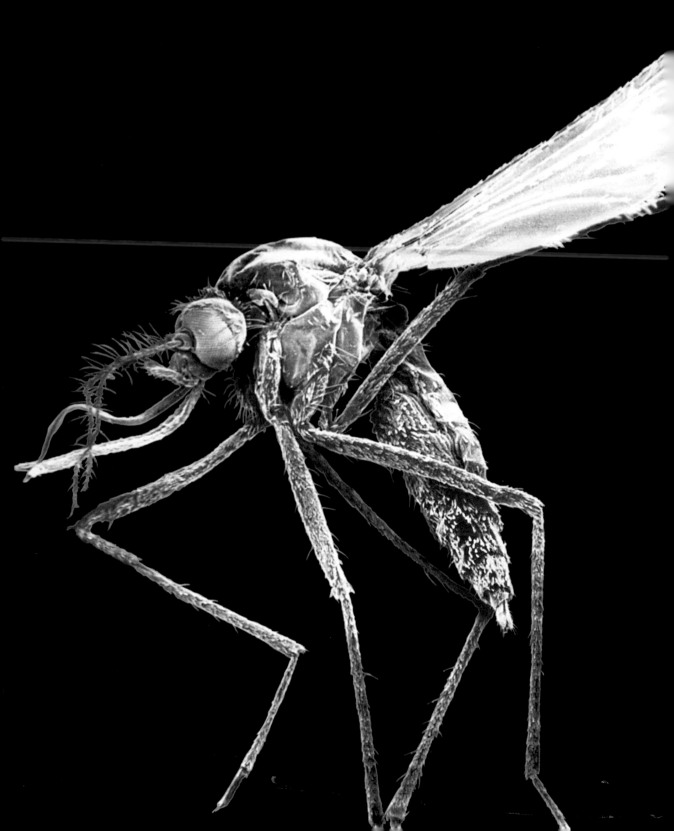

CHAPTER 3

VIRAL DISEASES:
MOSQUITO-BORNE KILLERS

Not really dead, yet not quite alive, viruses are the zombies of the microscopic world. They don't need food or water. They can't move or reproduce by themselves. They don't even need oxygen to survive. Unless they find the right animal or human host, viruses exist in a kind of suspended animation. They're much smaller than bacteria. If a single bacterium were the size of a basketball, a virus would be the size of a marble. Millions of viruses could fit inside the period at the end of this sentence.

Viruses are made of one or more strands of genetic material—either DNA or ribonucleic acid (RNA). The genetic material is surrounded by a protective protein shell called a capsid. Some viruses also have an outer fatty lipid envelope. Tiny protrusions on the capsid allow the virus to latch onto special sites on host cells. Scientists classify viruses by whether they use DNA or RNA for replication, and by their structure—whether they have a capsid or a lipid envelope. About four thousand viruses have been divided into about seventy families, while hundreds more remain unclassified. Viruses come in many shapes, but most are spherical or cylindrical shaped. No one is sure how long viruses have been on Earth, but it has been a very long time.

While some bacteria live in harmony with people and even perform useful tasks, viruses don't seem to be of any use to us.

Mosquitos are carriers for many diseases including West Nile virus, yellow fever, and malaria.

Viruses have only one purpose—to invade and take over the reproductive machinery of a plant or animal cell. After the protrusions on the capsid attach to the host cell, the virus enters by fusing its membrane with the cell's membrane, sort of like two soap bubbles touching. The virus injects its own genetic material into the host cell, forcing the host cell to produce copies of the virus. Soon the damaged host cell ruptures and releases thousands of new viruses. These in turn infect thousands of other host cells. The whole process, from assault and invasion to the release of new viruses, takes between one hour and one day.

The genetic material of any organism contains mutations passed on from previous generations. Because viruses reproduce quickly, any virus that contains a mutation giving it an advantage over other viruses will quickly pass that mutation to a new generation of viruses. Some mutations give viruses new ways to survive, such as the ability to infect a new plant or animal species.

Many viruses are transmitted to humans by way of an animal host, known as a vector. Mosquitoes carry some of the most widespread viral diseases in the world, including dengue fever, West Nile virus, and yellow fever.

Viruses enter our body through breaks in the skin and through the mucous membranes of the mouth, nose, and genitals. They make people sick because they destroy healthy cells or cause them to malfunction. Sometimes the host's body attacks its own cells to get rid of the virus infecting them. In other cases, viral DNA attaches to the host cell's DNA and is passed on to new generations of cells. Viruses may lurk inside host cells, invisible to the immune system, waiting for favorable conditions before springing into action.

A VIRUS
(cross section)

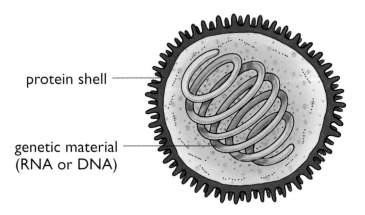

protein shell

genetic material
(RNA or DNA)

Because viruses live inside host cells, medications such as antibiotics cannot reach them. That makes viral infections difficult to cure. A relatively new class of medications called antiviral medications makes it harder for viruses to turn our cells into virus-making factories. But these medications can help prevent or cure only a few viral diseases. For example, antiviral medications are especially effective against viruses that cause influenza, but they don't work against West Nile virus.

Vaccines can prevent some viral diseases such as measles and polio. They can prevent or decrease the severity of the flu. We don't, however, have vaccines to prevent many other viral diseases, such as the ones that cause the common cold or AIDS. Fortunately, over the centuries, our bodies have learned to recognize many invading viruses. A healthy immune system can fight off or destroy these viruses.

west nile virus

In the late summer and early fall of 1999, dozens of people in New York City fell ill with fever, headache, and backache. A few developed encephalitis, a sudden swelling of the brain that can cause seizures and coma. Doctors suspected the outbreak was due to St. Louis encephalitis (SLE), a viral disease carried by mosquitoes. Meanwhile, veterinarians at the Bronx Zoo noticed that many of their exotic birds were dying. And hundreds of dead crows littered city streets. But SLE doesn't kill birds. After another month of testing, disease experts determined that the illness was caused by a mosquito-borne virus never before seen in the United States. West Nile virus had reached our shores.

First identified in Uganda in 1937, West Nile virus (WNV) is common in parts of Africa, Asia, and the Middle East. The virus normally lives in the blood of animals and birds. When a mosquito bites one of these infected animals, it carries WNV to other birds and animals. Researchers think WNV may have traveled to the United States in the blood of an infected bird. Or a mosquito might have hitched a ride in the cargo hold of a plane. Health officials hoped the virus would die out over the winter of 1999. But the disease returned with a vengeance the next year, and it looks like it's here to stay.

Since 1999 WNV has winged its way westward and southward from New York, carried in the blood of infected migratory birds. As of September 2005, the virus had been found in humans, animals, or birds in every state except Alaska and Hawaii. The virus is steadily moving northward into Canada and southward into Central America, putting large numbers of people and other animals at risk. WNV is especially deadly for birds. Tracking dead birds provides health officials with an early warning system to monitor the spread of the virus. When large numbers of dead birds are found, human cases of WNV are likely to follow.

WNV has been found in 230 species of American animals, including 130 kinds of birds. Mosquitoes don't feast only on human blood. Birds and other animals are tormented by mosquitoes. If an animal or bird is infected with WNV, a mosquito that bites it ingests the virus along with its blood meal. WNV is most likely to strike in late summer and early fall, when warm, damp conditions cause an increase in mosquito populations. In warmer climates where mosquitoes can breed year-round, WNV may strike at any time.

This research scientist from the Florida Department of Health tests a dead crow for West Nile virus. A clear shield and protective gloves help prevent her from contracting the disesase.

The human case count in the United States for the years 2002, 2003, and 2004 (as of June 30, 2005) was 16,500, including about 635 deaths (nearly four out of every hundred cases). There's no telling where WNV will strike hardest. In the first year, only New York was affected. By 2002 Illinois, Michigan, and Ohio had the most cases. Residents of Colorado, Nebraska, and South Dakota were stricken most often in 2003. And in 2004, WNV hit California the hardest, with Arizona and Colorado a distant second and third.

About eight out of ten people bitten by a mosquito infected with WNV have no symptoms of the disease. Most of the others will develop a mild, flulike illness five to fifteen days later. Symptoms include fever, headache, rash, muscle aches, swollen glands, abdominal pain, and vomiting. The illness lasts about one week, although fatigue hangs on a lot longer.

About one out of a hundred people with WNV becomes seriously ill with encephalitis or meningitis (swelling of the thin membranes that surround the brain and spinal cord). People with encephalitis or meningitis suffer severe headaches, backaches, and stiff necks. Complications include high fever, confusion, seizures, coma, and even death. A few people who survive the most serious form of WNV are left with paralyzed arms or legs. Northern California was hard hit in 2005, with large numbers of human cases.

West Nile virus can infect both humans and animals.

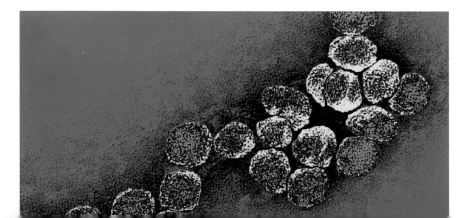

SENTINEL CHICKENS

Did you know that chickens are an important part of the nation's public health system? Mosquitoes bite all kinds of birds. If a mosquito carries WNV, the birds it bites, especially large birds like crows, magpies, and jays, may sicken and die. But for some reason, the virus doesn't make chickens sick. Instead, chickens produce antibodies, substances formed in the blood to help fight off invading organisms.

Many states maintain flocks of chickens to detect the presence of virus-carrying mosquitoes in the area. These chickens are called sentinels because they're like guards that warn of a coming attack. Every week the chickens' blood is tested for antibodies. If antibodies to WNV are found, health officials can warn the public about a possible outbreak.

Don't feel sorry for the sentinel chickens, though. At the end of the year, they retire with honors and a flock of younger chickens takes their place!

Scientists monitor chickens' blood for high levels of a certain protein, which indicates the presence of West Nile virus.

WNV killed hundreds of thousands of birds in the region, threatening the existence of the yellow-billed magpie, a species unique to the area.

Doctors should suspect WNV when people living in mosquito-infested areas get sick. Antibodies to WNV appear in blood and spinal fluid shortly after infection. There isn't a cure for WNV yet, but most people recover. Supportive care includes intravenous fluids (injected directly into a vein), pain relievers, and sometimes antibiotics to prevent secondary bacterial infections. WNV is not spread by normal person-to-person contact, but it has been passed in breast milk, transplanted organs, and blood transfusions.

In April 2005, scientists announced a trial of a new type of experimental human vaccine for WNV. A few healthy volunteers will receive three injections of the vaccine to determine if it's safe. If it is, the vaccine will then be tested on a larger group of people to see if it prevents WNV. Also in April 2005, another group of scientists announced that an experimental treatment cures WNV in mice. It will be a couple of years before this treatment is tested in people. Until a vaccine to prevent WNV or a medication to cure it becomes available, do your best to avoid being bitten by mosquitoes.

yellow fever

Wives were deserted by husbands, and children by parents. . . . The chambers of disease were deserted and the sick left to die of negligence. None could be found to remove the lifeless bodies. Their remains, suffered to decay by piecemeal, filled the air with deadly exhalations, and added tenfold to the devastation.
—Charles Brockden Brown,
describing an outbreak in Philadelphia in 1793

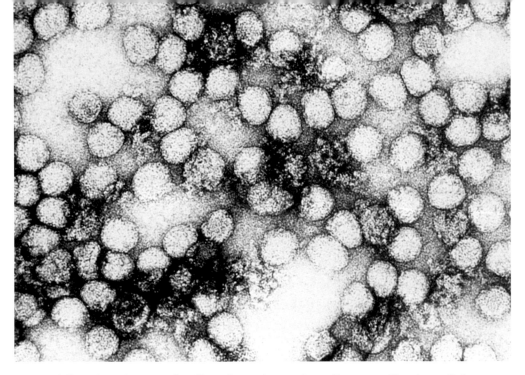

This virus is named yellow fever due to jaundice, or yellowing of the skin, which afflicts some people who contract the disease.

Yellow fever originated in the jungles of Africa, when mosquitoes carried the virus from sick monkeys to humans. It reached the Western Hemisphere about five hundred years ago, when slave ships brought infected people to the New World. After local mosquitoes fed on the blood of the new arrivals, they carried yellow fever to coastal towns in the United States, and to South America and Mexico.

A major U.S. epidemic of yellow fever occurred in 1793. It raged like wildfire through Philadelphia, then the nation's capital. President George Washington fled the city with his family. By the time the epidemic petered out in October of that year, one out of ten residents of Philadelphia had died. In 1900 U.S. Army surgeon Walter Reed discovered the link between mosquitoes and yellow fever. Public health officials then cleared out swamps where mosquitoes bred. The disease rapidly declined in North America.

Scientists have discovered several species of monkeys and apes in both Africa and South America that carry the virus without getting sick. But other monkeys are readily killed by yellow fever. Not only is the virus spread by mosquito bites, it can also be carried inside mosquito eggs. This means that a natural reservoir of yellow fever virus exists in nature—an insect, bird, or other animal that normally harbors the virus without getting sick. In these circumstances, it's nearly impossible to completely eliminate the disease.

Yellow fever remains endemic in tropical areas of Africa, Central and South America, and the Caribbean. It sickens at least 200,000 people a year and kills 30,000 of them. Yellow fever is considered a reemerging infectious disease. One reason it continues to spread is that people are cutting down the world's forests. Mosquitoes then move from their natural breeding grounds in the forests into villages, towns, and cities, carrying the yellow fever virus along with them. Yellow fever could return to warmer parts of the United States if U.S. mosquitoes bite infected tourists visiting the United States.

The initial symptoms of yellow fever—headache, backache, and fever—resemble those of many other illnesses. About 15 percent of people go on to develop a severe form of the disease, which damages the liver. When the liver is damaged, the skin and whites of the eyes turn yellow. That's what gave yellow fever the nickname Yellow Jack. People can hemorrhage (bleed) from the mouth or nose, or into internal organs. The sickest people spew out black vomit containing partially digested blood. People who survive yellow fever are immune to future attacks.

No specific cure for yellow fever exists. Patients receive intravenous fluids and medication to lower their fevers. Fortunately, most people recover. A safe and effective vaccine to prevent yellow fever has been in use for nearly seventy years. The virus that causes yellow fever is cultured in egg embryos before it is made into a vaccine. It is the only vaccine other than the influenza vaccine that is made in eggs. People who are allergic to eggs should not receive the vaccine, nor should people with faulty immune systems.

Most of the yellow fever deaths in the world could be prevented by vaccination. According to the World Health Organization, at least 80 percent of a population must be vaccinated in order to eliminate the spread of a disease like yellow fever. Many poor countries cannot afford to vaccinate this many of their citizens. In other cases, people refuse to be vaccinated or live in remote areas where the vaccine is not available.

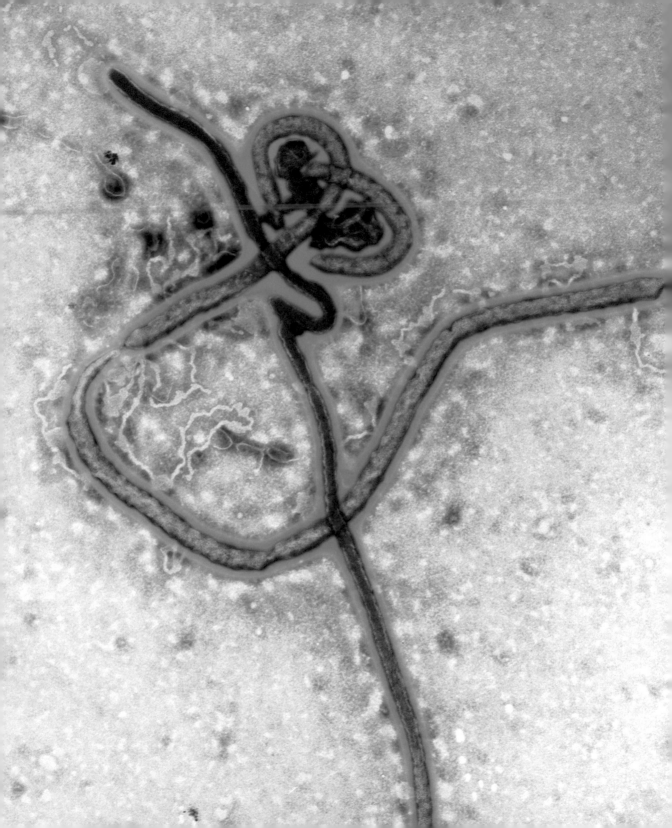

CHAPTER 4

MORE VIRUSES:
MICE, MONKEYS, BLOOD, AND AIR

Mosquitoes aren't the only creatures that carry viral diseases to people. Whenever animals and humans come into contact with each other, the potential for viral infection exists. For example, some viruses are passed to humans by contact with infected rodents. In many cases, the natural animal hosts do not get sick from the virus. Like humans, animals' immune systems help to keep viruses under control.

Some viruses, such as the one that causes AIDS, are passed by contact with infected blood and bodily secretions. The hemorrhagic fevers (such as Ebola) begin when humans come into contact with the blood or fluids of infected animals. The virus then passes from person to person through bodily contact. Influenza viruses generally travel from birds to pigs and then to humans. Once inside the human body, influenza viruses are easily passed from person to person by coughing and sneezing.

hantavirus

In May 1993, a young Navajo man died on the way to the Indian Medical Center in Gallup, New Mexico. He'd been sick for a few

The Ebola virus is named after the Ebola River in the Democratic Republic of the Congo where the first known outbreak of the disease occurred in 1976.

days with what he thought was the flu. At first, doctors suspected plague, but tests were negative for the plague bacterium. Over the next few weeks, other people in the region developed severe breathing problems. About half of them died. Scientists finally identified a previously unrecognized hantavirus as the culprit. Scientists knew hantavirus caused serious illnesses in other countries, but they'd never seen it attack the lungs like this. Researchers called the new hantavirus Sin Nombre virus. The disease it caused was named hantavirus pulmonary syndrome (HPS).

Hantavirus is part of the bunyavirus family. While it was officially discovered in 1993, Navajo medical tradition tells of mice carrying an illness older than plague. Elders remembered outbreaks in 1918 and 1933—both years with unusually heavy rainfall. The increase in rainfall caused trees in the region to produce great numbers of pinecones, which are a source of food for the region's mice. More food means more mice. With more mice around, people are more likely to come into contact with the mice and their droppings. The 1993 El Niño weather pattern caused another year of particularly heavy rain.

Because researchers knew that rodents in other countries carried hantavirus, they decided to look to rodents for the source of the new virus. Hundreds of mice and rats in the American Southwest were captured and sent to the CDC. About one-third of the deer mice tested positive for Sin Nombre virus, even though most of them appeared to be healthy.

Hantavirus infects people when they come into contact with the dried feces, urine, or saliva of rodents carrying it. Touching the animals or their droppings is not the only way to get sick. When the droppings and fluids dry up, tiny pieces float in the

Deer mice can carry hantavirus. The infected mice spread the disease when they are in close contact with people.

air with dust. This process is called aerosolization. Inhaling the infected dust can cause HPS.

As of July 2005, a total of 389 cases of HPS had been reported in the United States. That may not seem like many, but more than one-third of the people who get HPS die. It's possible that additional cases weren't correctly diagnosed. HPS tends to hit younger people more often than older ones, because younger people are more likely to be around rodents while working outdoors or cleaning house. The disease has been found in thirty states. New Mexico has had the most cases with California, Arizona, and Colorado running a distant second.

People start feeling sick one to five weeks after exposure to HPS-infected rodents. Early symptoms include fever, fatigue, and muscle aches in the hips and back. Some people have abdominal pain, vomiting, and diarrhea. HPS quickly progresses to coughing and breathing problems as fluid builds up in the lungs. Once the lungs begin to fail, shock sets in and people can die in as little as twenty-four hours.

There's no cure for HPS. Doctors treat symptoms with oxygen and medications to help clear the lungs and maintain blood pressure. The sickest patients must be put on a ventilator—a machine that breathes for them. Doctors may give antibiotics to prevent bacterial infections that can set in when HPS weakens the immune system. Many people get well on their own, although full recovery can take months.

We have no vaccine to prevent HPS. The best way to avoid HPS is to keep away from mice. Set out traps if you've seen signs of rodents. Clean up after them with diluted bleach while wearing a face mask. Pets don't carry hantavirus, but they may bring infected rodents into the house. Use care when disposing of rodents. Anyone who gets sick after being around rodents should see a doctor right away.

hemorrhagic fevers

In 1967 three laboratory workers at a large drug-making company in Marburg, Germany, thought they had an unusual case of the summer flu. But within days they became terribly ill, with high fevers and enlarged spleens. Their skin turned red and began peeling off their bodies. Then came the bleeding from every body opening. Day after day, more laboratory workers from the same company fell ill. Other lab workers in Frankfurt, Germany, and a veterinarian in Belgrade, Yugoslavia, developed the same symptoms. Some family members and health-care workers caught the disease as well. Despite receiving excellent care, seven of the thirty-one people who got this strange new virus died.

You may have heard about Ebola. Ebola is one of several deadly viruses called viral hemorrhagic fevers (VHFs). These viruses are among the most dangerous viruses known. VHFs include Ebola, Lassa, and Marburg fevers. Ebola and Marburg have unusual, threadlike shapes, and they're classified as filoviruses. Most VHFs didn't pose much of a threat to humans until we began encroaching on previously wild habitats and coming into contact with animals from those areas.

 ## marburg

Often, new diseases are first identified in exotic, remote regions. No one expected a new killer virus to turn up in modern Europe! It didn't take long to realize that all victims of Marburg had one thing in common—they had worked with imported African green monkeys. Investigators backtracked the shipments and learned that the monkeys had been trapped in

The green monkey is native to the woodlands and savannas of central and southern Africa. Green monkeys can carry Marburg virus.

the jungles of Uganda and shipped to Germany and Yugoslavia for research. Many had been dead on arrival.

WHO sent researchers into Uganda to find the source of the new virus. Scientists tested many kinds of monkeys and other primates. Only African green monkeys and red-tailed monkeys showed signs of active Marburg infection. Some chimpanzees and gorillas showed antibodies to Marburg, meaning the animals had been exposed to the virus but were not ill. Scientists speculated that Marburg virus had been infecting animals in Uganda for several years.

Researchers felt certain that the virus had a natural reservoir. Scientists tested hundreds of species of animal and insect life to determine the reservoir, but it was never found. No one knows where the virus lives between its periodic outbreaks.

Since the 1967 outbreak, additional cases of Marburg have occurred in Africa. The first big outbreak took place between 1998 and 2000 in the Democratic Republic of the Congo—154 people got sick and 128 of them died. A more serious outbreak began in Angola during 2004. As of September 2005, the WHO had reported 368 confirmed cases with a fatality rate of 88 percent, making Marburg one of the deadliest-known diseases.

Initially, a few people contracted Marburg by contact with infected animals, often by hunting and eating monkeys. When family members and health-care workers take care of people infected with Marburg, they can get the virus by coming into contact with infected bodily fluids such as blood, urine, saliva, vomit, feces, and semen. People can also become infected with the virus when they prepare the bodies of dead family members for burial.

People with Marburg start out with a high fever, severe headaches, and muscle aches. Next comes diarrhea, abdominal pain, nausea, and vomiting. A few days later, the hemorrhaging begins. The viruses destroy platelets (blood cells that prevent bleeding by helping blood to clot) and damage blood vessels. Blood seeps from the vessels. Patients bleed under the skin, inside internal organs, or from the mouth and rectum. The kidneys and liver can be permanently damaged. Seizures and coma may follow. Death occurs from loss of blood and from shock about nine days after the person gets sick.

Doctors have no specific cure or treatment for Marburg. Patients are given medications to help control the fever and bleeding. They receive intravenous fluids and other care to make them as comfortable as possible. Health-care workers and family members can decrease the risk of getting Marburg by avoiding contact with bodily fluids of sick people.

Marburg is highly infectious, so health-care workers must take precautions to protect themselves against the disease. This doctor is treating a Marburg patient in Angola.

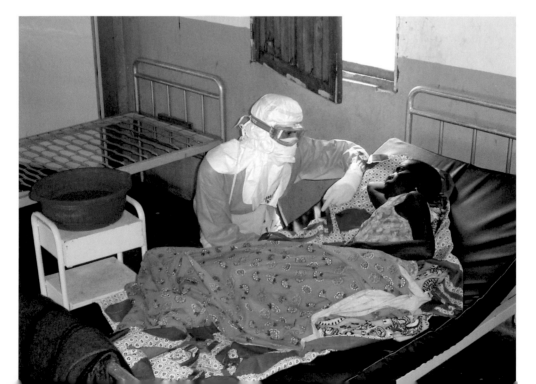

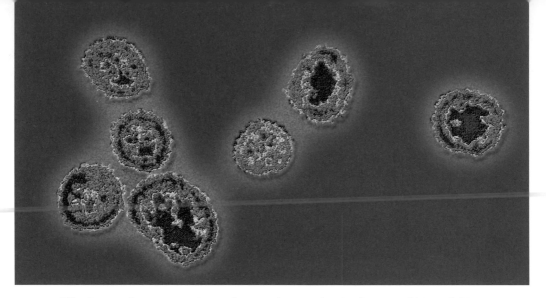

The Lassa virus causes Lassa fever, a hemorrhagic disease of West Africa.

lassa

Lassa fever was discovered in 1969, when two missionary nurses died in Lassa, Nigeria. The newly identified virus was named after the town. It has become a common disease in West Africa, especially in Guinea, Liberia, Nigeria, and Sierra Leone. The natural host of Lassa is a rat commonly found in homes and villages of the region. Lassa is part of the arenavirus family.

People get sick with Lassa fever when they come in contact with an infected rat's urine, feces, or saliva, similar to the way people contract hantavirus. When droppings dry up, tiny particles float in the air and can be inhaled. In addition, people sometimes eat infected rats. That's a sure way to get Lassa. Like Marburg, Lassa can also be transmitted by bodily fluids.

Lassa is much more common than Marburg and Ebola, but it's not as deadly. An estimated 300,000 people develop Lassa each year in West Africa, and about 5,000 die of it. In some African countries, up to 16 percent of people admitted to hospitals have Lassa fever.

Symptoms of Lassa begin one to three weeks after exposure to the virus. People may have fever, chest pain, sore throat, coughing, abdominal pain, vomiting, and diarrhea. Bleeding may come later, although it's not as severe as with Marburg. The virus may attack the nervous system, causing encephalitis and permanent hearing loss. Lassa is especially dangerous to pregnant women and their fetuses. The fetuses of 95 percent of women infected with Lassa die in the uterus.

No specific cure exists for Lassa. An antiviral drug called ribavirin may reduce the severity of symptoms in some people if given early. People can avoid getting infected by the virus that causes Lassa by ridding their homes of rodents and keeping food—which attracts rodents—in closed containers. Health-care workers and family members should use protective measures such as masks, gowns, and gloves when caring for patients with Lassa. Scientists haven't yet developed a vaccine to prevent Lassa.

ebola

Ebola was first recognized in the Democratic Republic of the Congo in 1976, and it was named after a river in the region. No one knows where the virus lives between outbreaks because scientists haven't found its natural host. Several kinds of monkeys and primates also get Ebola, but it's as deadly for them as it is for people.

Despite all the publicity Ebola receives, it remains a rare disease. Since 1976 doctors have confirmed only about 1,850 cases. Ebola kills about 65 percent of those it infects. When a disease such as Ebola or Marburg makes a person very sick, very quickly, that person doesn't live long enough to pass it on to many others.

As with Marburg, outbreaks of Ebola begin when a human comes into contact with a sick animal. When that person gets ill, family members and health-care workers can contract Ebola from the victim's blood or bodily secretions from infected needles. The symptoms of Ebola are similar to those of Marburg, and like Marburg, it has no specific treatment.

In 2005 scientists announced they had created two filovirus vaccines—one that prevented Ebola in monkeys and one that did the same for Marburg. Such results advance the development of human vaccines. A small human trial of a different experimental vaccine for Ebola began in 2004, but it will take a couple of years before the results are known. Someday the natural reservoirs of Ebola and Marburg may be discovered so that efforts to control the viruses can be undertaken.

human immunodeficiency virus

The thirty-three-year-old man stumbled into a clinic at the Los Angeles Medical Center. He was terribly thin and pale. He had a fever, a bad cough, and chest pain. A thick cottage-cheeselike substance grew on his tongue. Laboratory results showed that the man had a rare type of pneumonia caused by a fungus. The substance in his mouth was a yeast infection. He tested positive for cytomegalovirus. Perhaps the most troubling finding was the nearly complete absence of T cells in his blood. These white blood cells are key components of the immune system. Doctors had never seen such an unusual combination of problems in one person. Over the next few months, a dozen similar cases broke out in Los Angeles, San Francisco, and New York City. By early 1981, doctors who followed infectious diseases realized they were witnessing the dawn of a mysterious and deadly new disease.

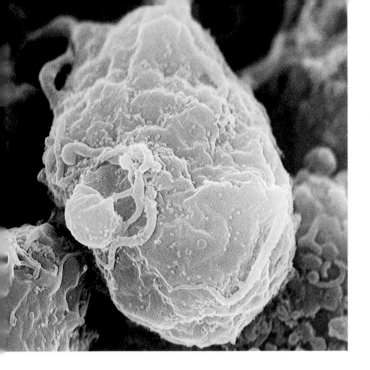

More than twenty years after it was discovered, HIV kills more people each year than any other infectious disease.

Scientists believe HIV first developed in humans when they ate or handled infected monkeys and chimpanzees in Africa. Recent genetic testing suggests HIV jumped the species barrier from animals to humans around 1930. Researchers have found HIV in stored blood from people who died years ago from what were then unknown causes.

HIV belongs to a family of viruses called retroviruses. Retroviruses' only genetic material is RNA. HIV contains two strands of RNA. Two major strains of HIV exist. HIV-1 is the primary cause of AIDS worldwide, while HIV-2 is found largely in West Africa. Although HIV-2 is less easily transmitted and it causes AIDS much less quickly than HIV-1, the two strains have much in common.

Like other viruses, HIV latches onto the wall of a host cell. It targets T cells. The virus invades the cell and forces it to make duplicate copies of itself. The virus gradually takes over and kills most of the T cells.

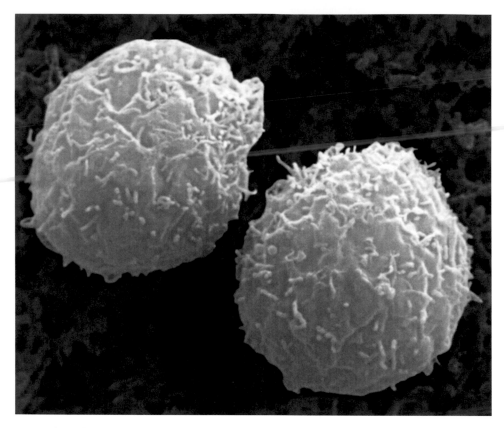

White blood cells form the main part of the immune system. They attempt to destroy all foreign microbes that enter the body.

People don't die from HIV itself. As the number of T cells decreases, the body loses the ability to fight off common infections that don't usually make people sick. These are called opportunistic infections—infections that people with normal immune systems can fight off. Such infections are often seen in patients undergoing treatment for cancer (such treatment weakens the immune system) or in people who have received organ transplants. Ultimately, it's one of these infections that causes death. About one-third of HIV patients die from TB infections.

Doctors say a person infected with HIV has AIDS when T cells drop to a dangerously low level and at least one opportunistic infection is present. Some of the infections HIV patients commonly develop include:

- *Pneumocystis:* a fungus that causes severe pneumonia in HIV patients
- Kaposi's sarcoma: a cancer of blood vessels caused by human herpes virus 8. It causes reddish-purple bumps on the skin. It can also grow on internal organs.
- *Candida:* a yeast that infects mucous membranes of the body (mouth, intestines, vagina, rectum)
- *Cryptosporidium parvum:* a parasite that causes severe diarrhea and weight loss
- *Cytomegalovirus:* a normally harmless virus that can attack the eyes, liver, lungs, and brain of HIV patients
- *Mycobacterium tuberculosis:* the bacterium that causes tuberculosis, which can be deadly for HIV patients

HIV is a global pandemic that continues to spread each year. It infects as many as 42 million people worldwide. In some parts of Africa, over one-third of adults have HIV or AIDS. In 2003 an estimated 2.9 million people died of AIDS, making it the most common cause of death by infectious disease. More than 20 million people have died of AIDS since it was first identified. In the United States, more than 1 million people were estimated to have HIV in 2003. The number of new cases among women and girls has increased dramatically, from 6 percent of all HIV cases in 1985 to 27 percent in 2003. In 2003 nearly five out of every one hundred persons infected with HIV were thirteen to twenty-four years old.

HIV is largely transmitted by sexual contact and by the use of infected needles. Thousands of people were infected by

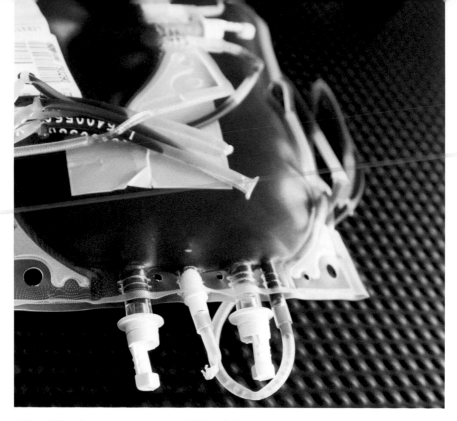

Blood banks screen donated blood for HIV as well as for several other diseases. This precaution helps prevent the spread of disease.

blood transfusions before blood banks began screening for HIV in 1985. Since screening began, this means of transmission has been virtually eliminated. While the virus has been found in saliva, tears, urine, and nasal secretions, no cases of HIV transmission by these fluids have been documented.

Several weeks after infection with HIV, people develop a mild illness with fever, headache, and swollen glands. These symptoms last one or two weeks. Years may pass before an HIV-infected person feels sick enough to seek medical care. But people are contagious during this asymptomatic (without symptoms) period. They can pass HIV on to others long before realizing they have it. That's what makes unprotected sex so dangerous.

Left untreated, HIV usually leads to AIDS and death within a few years due to opportunistic infections. There isn't a cure for HIV/AIDS, although some medications slow the virus's copying process. Others slow the release of new HIV viruses into the bloodstream. A carefully chosen combination of medications can drastically reduce the number of viruses in the body and make patients feel much better. With treatment, people may enjoy relatively healthy lives despite having HIV. But no one knows how long the medications will work. HIV is constantly mutating and becoming ever more resistant to medications. Unlike many other infectious agents, HIV can change drastically within one person during the course of infection. Medications that once worked for that person become less effective over time.

People infected with HIV/AIDS must also take medications to control opportunistic infections as they arise. The opportunistic infections caused by fungi, other viruses, and bacteria such as TB are also likely to become resistant to medications.

Scientists do not yet have a vaccine to prevent HIV infection, although they have been working on it for twenty years. Several experimental vaccines are being tested for safety on small numbers of people. If the vaccines prove safe, they will be tested in thousands of people over several years to determine their effectiveness at preventing HIV infection. No one can say for sure whether an HIV vaccine will eventually become available. In the future, perhaps children will be immunized against HIV as routinely as they are vaccinated against measles and mumps.

Until there's a cure for HIV or a vaccine to prevent it, people must take important steps to decrease the risk of becoming infected. These include commonsense measures such as consistent practice of safe sex and avoiding the use of injectable drugs. Abuse of alcohol and drugs must also be avoided, because it can impair judgment and lead to risky behaviors.

influenza

These men start with what appears to be an ordinary attack of LaGrippe or influenza, and when brought to the hospital, they very rapidly develop the most vicious type of pneumonia that has ever been seen. It is only a matter of a few hours then until death comes and it is simply a struggle for air until they suffocate. It is horrible. An extra long barracks has been vacated for the use of the morgue. It would make any man sit up and take notice to walk down the long lines of dead soldiers all dressed and laid out in double rows.

—Dr. Roy Grist writing about the Spanish flu, September 29, 1918, Camp Devens, Massachusetts

Influenza, also called the flu, has been around for at least five hundred years. Scientists know that migrating aquatic birds such as ducks, geese, and gulls are the natural reservoirs for flu viruses. Most modern flu strains are believed to originate in China, where wild waterfowl freely mingle with domesticated chickens and ducks. The domesticated birds then come in contact with pigs, which live close to people in that part of the world. When pigs pick up the virus from birds, the virus's genes get shuffled, giving the virus the ability to infect humans.

Flu viruses are part of the orthomyxovirus family. Each virus carries eight strands of RNA within it. Flu viruses mutate extremely rapidly, which makes them a constant challenge for scientists and doctors.

You may have heard people say, "It's just the flu." The truth is, influenza can be a very serious illness. The worst pandemic of modern times was caused by the Spanish flu of 1918–1919. In just a few months, it killed at least 50 million people around the world, including hundreds of thousands of soldiers fighting in World War I (1914–1918). Flu killed four times as many people as died fighting in the war. While most flu strains target the youngest and oldest people, the Spanish flu killed millions of people in their prime adult years. It hit military bases and camps especially hard. People died in one or two days, sometimes in hours, from overwhelming pneumonia that turned their skin blue from lack of oxygen. People drowned in the bloody foam that poured from their lungs.

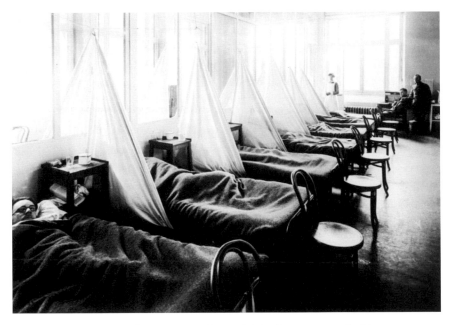

Soldiers lie in an influenza ward at a U.S. Army camp in France during World War I.

DISEASES AS WEAPONS OF WAR

A bioterrorism attack against the civilian population in the United States is inevitable in the twenty-first century. The only question is which agent will be used and under what circumstances will the attack occur.
—Anthony S. Fauci, MD, director, National Institute of Allergy and Infectious Diseases, September 2000

The word *bioterrorism* became part of our vocabulary in October 2001, after someone sent deadly anthrax spores through the U.S. mail. Experts define bioterrorism as "the deliberate, planned, and unnatural reemergence of pathogenic microbes in settings designed to cause maximal suffering and death"

The CDC has ranked bacteria and viruses according to the risk they pose to national security. The following Category A microbes are the most dangerous because they could be easily distributed, are readily transmitted among people, result in high mortality, and are likely to cause panic:

Anthrax bacteria occur naturally in soil and can infect cattle and sheep. People may get anthrax by handling infected animal hides and wool. People infected this way, however, are unlikely to get inhalation anthrax, the deadliest form of the disease. Anthrax is the most likely choice for a bioterrorism attack because its hard spores can be aerosolized. In this form, a few pounds of spores released from a plane and distributed through the air could kill half of the people it infects. Antibiotics are used to treat anthrax. An effective vaccine is routinely given to members of the military and certain laboratory workers.

Botulism bacteria live in soil and are transmitted in food and water. The toxin produced by the bacteria is the most poisonous substance known. If bioterrorists released .04 ounce (1 gram)—the weight of a paper clip—of the spores in aerosolized form, they could kill one million people. An antitoxin is available to treat botulism infections.

Plague bacteria live in rodents and are spread by fleas. Once infected, humans can spread the disease from person to person. Plague killed at least one-third of Europe's population in the fourteenth century. WHO estimates that if 110 pounds (50 kilograms) of plague bacteria were released over a large city, about 250,000 people would be killed. Antibiotics work against the bacterium, but no vaccine exists to prevent the disease.

Smallpox has killed more people throughout history than all other diseases combined. Currently the virus is believed to exist only in two laboratories, one in the United States and one in Russia. There is no cure for smallpox. The vaccine used to prevent infection was so effective at eliminating the disease from the world that people are no longer immunized against it. Only members of the military and certain laboratory workers receive the vaccination.

Tularemia bacteria are carried by small mammals such as rabbits and squirrels. People can get tularemia in several ways, including inhaling aerosolized bacteria or being bitten by an infected insect. It's highly contagious. Inhaling just 10 bacteria can make a person sick. Tularemia can be treated with antibiotics. The vaccine to prevent tularemia is given only to certain laboratory workers.

Viral hemorrhagic fevers such as Ebola, Lassa, and Marburg pose a risk as agents of bioterrorism because the viruses are highly lethal and the diseases, for the most part, cannot be cured or prevented.

Public health officials are preparing for the possibility of a bioterrorist attack in several ways. First responders—paramedics, police, firefighters, doctors, and nurses—have received special training. The government is stockpiling vaccines and medications to be used against diseases such as anthrax and smallpox. Federal, state, and local authorities have developed emergency plans for dealing with the release of deadly infectious organisms. Also, many diseases must be reported to the CDC; this allows health officials to identify abnormal patterns. For example, an outbreak of plague in the southwestern United States might be normal. But an outbreak of plague in New York City might signal a bioterrorist attack.

Other lesser flu pandemics that circled the globe were the Asian flu in 1957 and the Hong Kong flu in 1968.

Flu infects one or two people out of ten in the United States each year. It sends about 100,000 people to the hospital and kills about 50,000 of them. Flu kills up to half a million people around the world annually. It is highly contagious. Flu viruses are passed through the air when an infected person talks, coughs, or sneezes. A sneeze can leave a 25-foot (7.6-meter) cloud of infectious flu viruses hanging in the air for fifteen minutes! Anyone who walks through that invisible cloud will breathe in flu viruses. They immediately set up housekeeping in the airways and lungs. The viruses can also live for hours on cold, hard surfaces such as doorknobs and faucets. When people touch one of those surfaces and then touch their eyes or mouth, the virus enters their bodies.

Influenza causes fever, weakness, headaches, muscle aches, coughing, and chest pain. Compared to cold symptoms, flu symptoms come on much more suddenly, are more severe, and last longer. It can take two to three weeks for healthy people to completely recover from the flu. Sometimes people say, "I've got the stomach flu." Influenza is a respiratory disease and has nothing to do with what we call the "stomach flu." While many viruses, bacteria, and parasites can cause nausea, vomiting, and diarrhea, those are seldom flu symptoms.

Flu vaccines are highly effective in preventing or decreasing the severity of flu. Because flu viruses change so rapidly, scientists must make a different vaccine each year to fight the predicted strains of virus. For this reason, people need to get vaccinated against the flu every year to be protected from the disease. Flu shots usually are given in October and November. During the 2004–2005 flu season, only half the expected doses of vaccine were available. British health officials suspended the license of one of the flu vaccine's main manufacturers. The company destroyed millions of doses that were potentially contaminated. Many people who should have been vaccinated weren't. Fortunately, it was a fairly mild flu season.

While no cure exists for the flu, several new antiviral medications help. They may prevent flu, although they're not as effective as flu shots. Taken within forty-eight hours of the appearance of symptoms, they help people recover more quickly. During flu season, do what you can to stay away from sick people, and ask your doctor if the flu vaccine (available by injection or nasal spray) is a good idea for you.

Until recently, scientists believed people couldn't get flu directly from birds. They thought it had to pass through such animals as pigs first. But in 1997, a flu virus called avian, or bird, flu leaped directly from chickens to humans in Hong

Thai soldiers collect chickens during the 2004 avian flu epidemic. The birds were killed to prevent the spread of the disease.

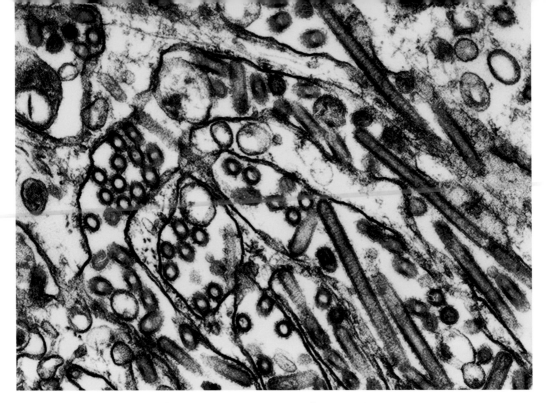

The blue areas of this image are avian influenza viruses.

Kong, killing one-third of those it infected. Alarmed health officials ordered the immediate slaughter of 1.4 million chickens to halt the contagion. That seemed to work for a while.

But in 2004, bird flu broke out again. It first appeared in millions of birds, then in dozens of people who ate or handled infected birds. By September 2005, the outbreak had killed about half of the 112 people diagnosed with bird flu. While most cases of bird flu have been in Vietnam and Thailand, infected birds have been found in nine or ten other countries. Bird flu does not easily pass from one person to another. But health officials around the world predict that it's only a matter of time until the virus mutates so that it is more contagious. If that happens, health officials say, the world could be in for another flu pandemic.

severe acute respiratory syndrome

A young Chinese woman visited Hong Kong in late February 2003. A few days later, she got a fever and a dry cough. She felt well enough to travel, so she went on to Singapore. On March 1, she was admitted to a hospital there. A chest X ray showed pneumonia, but tests for the bacteria and viruses that cause pneumonia were negative. Her fever soared to 104°F (40°C), and she needed oxygen. Liver problems developed. Antibiotics had no effect. It took nearly two weeks for her to recover. Doctors hadn't known that the woman was contagious, but in the next two weeks, twenty people who had been near her in the hospital came down with the same illness. The new patients were healthy and young, averaging about twenty-eight years old. Most got better, but three of them died.

Severe acute respiratory syndrome (SARS) was the first truly new disease of the twenty-first century to show up in humans. The first-known human case was identified in November 2002. The last case of the outbreak occurred in June 2003. Researchers discovered the cause and source of SARS in record time. The virus that causes SARS is a member of the coronavirus family, related to the common cold. Scientists traced its source back to several wild animals common to South China—masked palm civets, raccoon dogs, and Chinese ferret badgers. But not all researchers were sure that these animals were natural hosts for the virus. Late in 2005, scientists announced that Chinese horseshoe bats are probably the reservoir for the SARS virus. Bats are eaten in parts of Asia, and their feces are used to make folk medicines. Keeping people and food animals away from these bats may help prevent a future SARS outbreak.

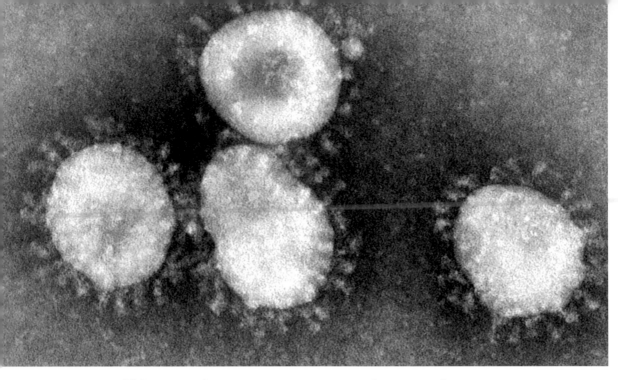

This coronavirus causes severe acute respiratory syndrome.

Researchers believe the virus crossed over to humans late in 2002, when infected animals were caught and sold in live food markets. Antibodies to the virus were found in the blood of healthy animal handlers, showing they'd been exposed to SARS. Once the virus crossed from animals to humans, it began to pass from one person to another. SARS is spread through the air and by touching contaminated objects, much like flu viruses.

By the time the SARS outbreak was over, the virus had spread along international air routes to thirty-three countries, including the United States. An estimated 8,450 people developed SARS, and about 810 of them died. SARS killed nearly 1 out of 10 people it infected, making it deadlier than the flu. Fortunately, SARS is less contagious than influenza. SARS infected twenty-seven people in the United States, but none of them died. It seemed to cause a milder illness here than in Asia.

Like many respiratory illnesses, SARS starts with fever, headache, and body aches. A few days later, patients develop a dry cough. Some may need oxygen or have to be put on a ventilator. Even though there is no treatment for SARS, most people recover. Some of the sickest patients who recover are left with lung damage that causes ongoing breathing problems.

On July 5, 2003, WHO reported the human-to-human chain of transmission for SARS had been broken and that it had been banished from its human host. Yet a few people have since become infected with SARS through laboratory accidents or by handling infected animals. Scientists were surprised that the newer cases showed the SARS virus had mutated significantly since the 2002–2003 outbreak.

In 2004 experimental vaccines succeeded at preventing SARS in mice and monkeys. By the middle of 2005, two promising vaccines were being tested in humans, one in the United States and the other in China. Health experts say it's impossible to know if or when another outbreak of SARS will occur. Because it's a strong possibility, work on developing a vaccine to prevent the disease will continue. The SARS outbreak showed that when countries work together, a dangerous, new infectious disease can quickly be identified and controlled.

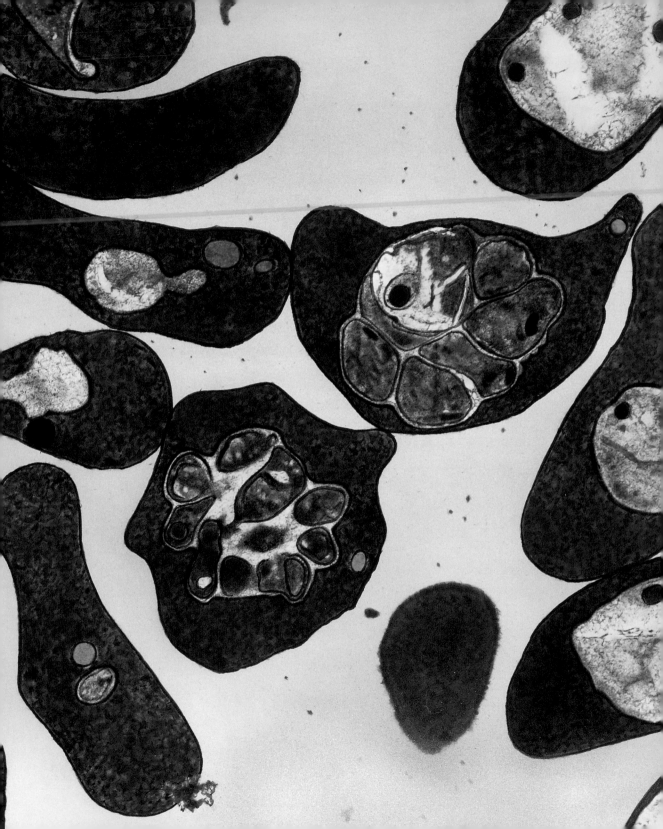

CHAPTER 5

PARASITES AND PRIONS:
DANGEROUS AND DEADLY

Parasites are organisms that live in or on other organisms. The mistletoe that hangs in your doorway at Christmas is a parasite that damages its host tree by stealing its nutrients. The ticks and fleas that plague our pets are parasites that live on the blood they suck from the animals. A hundred different parasites are known to infect humans, including a 30-foot-long (9 m) tapeworm that lodges in the gut so it can guzzle predigested food and the microscopic malaria parasite that ruptures our red blood cells as it reproduces. Parasites come in many different forms and live in a wide variety of places. What they all have in common is that they get their food and shelter from their host organisms.

malaria

In the summer of 1999, two eleven-year-old boys from New York City went to Baiting Hollow Boy Scout Camp on Long Island. They explored the woods and marshes around their camp, slapping at the mosquitoes that constantly dive-bombed them. A few days after they returned home, both boys got fevers and shaking chills. It didn't take long for doctors to make the diagnosis—they had malaria. Even with treatment, they'll likely suffer from fevers off and on for years.

These red blood cells are infected with the parasite that causes malaria. Parasites are mutiplying in the two cells in the center. Eventually the cells will burst, releasing parasites into the bloodstream.

The parasite that causes malaria is a protozoan (a microscopic, single-celled organism) called *Plasmodium*. It has a complex life cycle that requires both human and mosquito hosts. When an infected mosquito bites someone, it injects saliva into the bloodstream. The saliva carries sporozoites, the infectious stage of the malaria parasite, which travel through the blood to the liver. Each sporozoite invades a liver cell and devours the cell's contents. Then the sporozoite splits into merozoites. Thousands of merozoites burst out of the liver. They travel to red blood cells and gobble up hemoglobin (the iron-containing protein in red blood cells that carries oxygen to the body). Merozoites grow, split, and spew out new merozoites that invade other red blood cells over and over again.

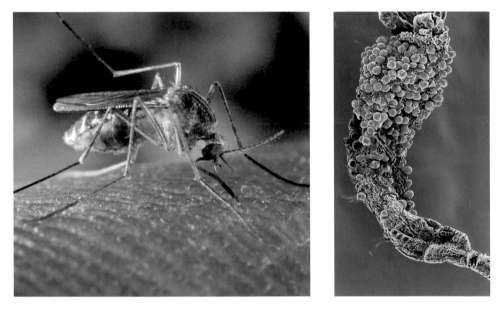

Mosquitoes (left) transmit malaria when they bite an animal or person. Malaria parasites are viewed on the stomach wall of a mosquito (right). The parasites are at an early stage of their life cycle.

Some of the merozoites morph into a reproductive stage called gametocytes. When another mosquito bites the infected person, gametocytes are sucked into the mosquito's stomach. The gametocytes produce male and female reproductive cells that undergo sexual reproduction and become zygotes (fertilized eggs). Each zygote divides into many new sporozoites that travel to the mosquito's salivary glands, ready to be injected into the next human host.

Malaria has plagued humans for thousands of years. The ancient Egyptians wrote about malaria epidemics. The Greek physician Hippocrates described the disease in detail. Some historians think malaria might have contributed to the fall of the Roman Empire. Malaria caused more sick time for U.S. soldiers in World War II (1939–1945) and the Vietnam War (1957–1975) than did combat injuries.

Malaria is no stranger to the United States. In the first part of the twentieth century, more than half a million Americans contracted malaria every year. During World War II, the U.S. government established an office in Atlanta, Georgia, to help protect soldiers training in the region from malaria. The Centers for Disease Control and Prevention grew out of that project.

If the WHO had a most-wanted list, malaria would be among the top three, along with HIV and TB. More than one-third of the world's population lives in areas where malaria is endemic. It kills as many as 2.7 million of its victims each year. It's especially deadly to pregnant women and young children. In some regions, about one-third of people admitted to hospitals are there because of malaria. Nine out of ten malaria deaths occur in Africa, where the disease kills a child every thirty seconds.

Malaria's Cycle of Infection

Plasmodium, the protozoan that causes malaria, has a complex life cycle. It passes through several different stages within its mosquito and human hosts.

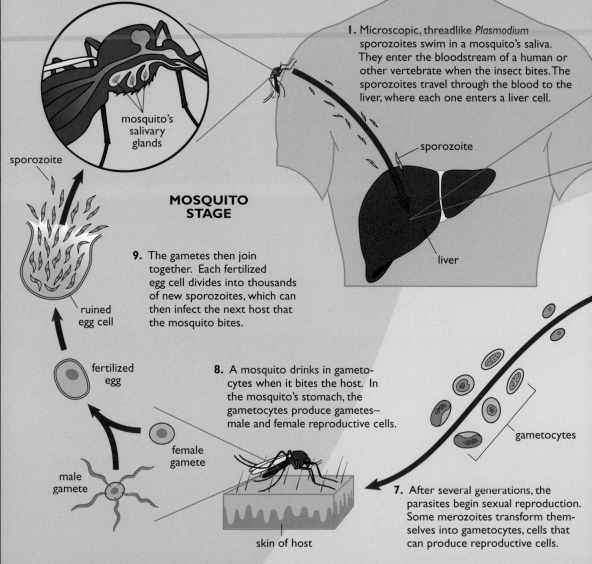

mosquito's salivary glands

sporozoite

1. Microscopic, threadlike *Plasmodium* sporozoites swim in a mosquito's saliva. They enter the bloodstream of a human or other vertebrate when the insect bites. The sporozoites travel through the blood to the liver, where each one enters a liver cell.

sporozoite

liver

MOSQUITO STAGE

9. The gametes then join together. Each fertilized egg cell divides into thousands of new sporozoites, which can then infect the next host that the mosquito bites.

ruined egg cell

fertilized egg

gametocytes

8. A mosquito drinks in gameto-cytes when it bites the host. In the mosquito's stomach, the gametocytes produce gametes— male and female reproductive cells.

female gamete

male gamete

skin of host

7. After several generations, the parasites begin sexual reproduction. Some merozoites transform them-selves into gametocytes, cells that can produce reproductive cells.

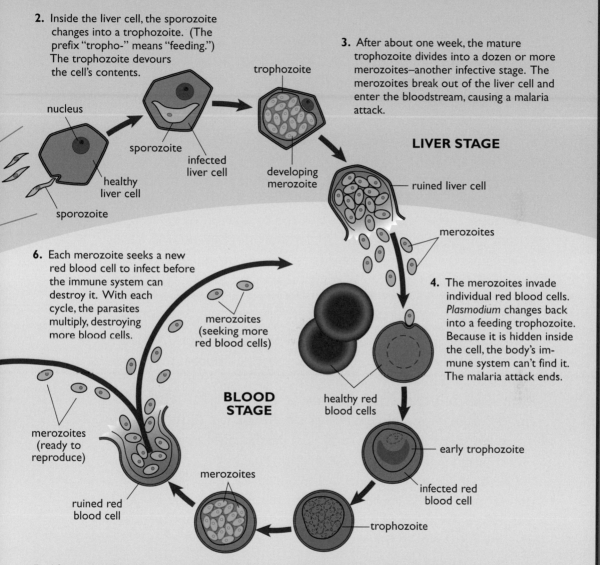

2. Inside the liver cell, the sporozoite changes into a trophozoite. (The prefix "tropho-" means "feeding.") The trophozoite devours the cell's contents.

nucleus

sporozoite

infected liver cell

healthy liver cell

sporozoite

trophozoite

developing merozoite

3. After about one week, the mature trophozoite divides into a dozen or more merozoites—another infective stage. The merozoites break out of the liver cell and enter the bloodstream, causing a malaria attack.

LIVER STAGE

ruined liver cell

merozoites

6. Each merozoite seeks a new red blood cell to infect before the immune system can destroy it. With each cycle, the parasites multiply, destroying more blood cells.

merozoites (seeking more red blood cells)

merozoites (ready to reproduce)

ruined red blood cell

merozoites

BLOOD STAGE

healthy red blood cells

4. The merozoites invade individual red blood cells. *Plasmodium* changes back into a feeding trophozoite. Because it is hidden inside the cell, the body's immune system can't find it. The malaria attack ends.

early trophozoite

infected red blood cell

trophozoite

5. After one to four days—depending on the species—the trophozoite again divides to form merozoites. The ruined red blood cell bursts open, spilling the merozoites and their wastes into the bloodstream. Perhaps because merozoites mature at a similar rate, they all break out of the blood cells at about the same time. The synchronized timing gives malaria its characteristic symptoms—bouts of chills and fever alternating with periods when the victim feels better.

Most people get malaria from the bite of an infected mosquito. However, it can also be transmitted by transfusion of infected blood or by sharing needles for drug injection. When a pregnant woman has malaria, parasites may pile up in the placenta (the organ that connects the mother and the fetus), impairing fetal nutrition. Many babies of malaria-infected mothers are miscarried or born dead. Those that survive are likely to be small and anemic.

People living in areas of endemic malaria are continually exposed. Some gradually build up immunity against the parasite. Those who aren't immune get sick ten to sixteen days after the bite of an infected mosquito. Malaria produces repeated cycles of chills, fever, and heavy sweats. It causes headaches, nausea, and vomiting. Sometimes parasites reach the brain, where they may lead to seizures and coma. Malaria can damage the liver and cause kidney failure. People feel the sickest when red blood cells burst open and release merozoites into the bloodstream.

Doctors diagnose malaria by finding the parasites in the blood. It used to be easy to treat malaria with the drug chloroquine. But many cases of malaria have become resistant to it, as well as several other medications. Sometimes a combination of medications is needed to treat malaria. If the disease damages large numbers of red blood cells, patients need blood transfusions.

Controlling malaria remains a major challenge. Not only has the parasite grown more resistant to medications, the mosquitoes that carry it are also growing more resistant to insecticides used to kill them.

The treatment and control of malaria is a global health priority because it affects the health of so many people. Scientists are constantly working to find new ways to fight the disease. One approach involves developing better methods of controlling the

A helicopter sprays a field in New Jersey with an insecticide that kills mosquitoes. Controlling the mosquito population helps prevent malaria.

mosquitoes that carry the parasite. The second way is to find better treatments for the disease itself, such as new medications to kill the parasite once it has invaded the human body.

Perhaps most important, scientists want to develop a vaccine to prevent the disease. But this is not easy. According to one researcher, "It is such a complex parasite, with two hosts and more than 5,300 genes...that it has coevolved with human beings and developed mechanisms to avoid the host immune system."

About one thousand cases of malaria are reported to the CDC in the United States every year. Over the past ten years, people in California, Florida, Michigan, New Jersey, New York, and Texas have come down with the disease. Most Americans who get malaria contract it in another country. A few, like the boys at the scout camp in New York, get it from mosquitoes that picked it up from infected travelers who returned to the United States. Someday it may be possible to prevent the misery caused by the malaria parasite. Until then, people traveling in areas where malaria is common should take precautions to avoid mosquitoes.

prions

Prions are unlike any infectious organism known to science. Strictly speaking, they aren't organisms at all. Prions have no DNA or RNA. They do not eat or reproduce, yet they do manage to make more of themselves. Heat cannot destroy prions nor can radiation. The word *prion* is an acronym for "proteinaceous infectious particle." A prion is a protein molecule that normally occurs in many parts of the body, and it appears in large numbers on the surface of nerve cells in the brain. For unknown reasons, a prion may fold into an abnormal shape. When such mutated prions touch normal proteins, they cause them to misfold as well.

Abnormal prions damage the brain, leaving it filled with spongelike holes, a condition called spongiform (spongelike) encephalopathy (brain disease). Formally known as transmissible spongiform encephalopathies, or TSEs, prion diseases are always fatal. TSEs cause a disease called scrapie in sheep, chronic wasting disease in deer and elk, and mad cow disease in cattle. A TSE also causes a rare disease called Creutzfeldt-Jakob disease (CJD) in humans. A new variation of CJD, known as vCJD, has landed on the list of emerging infectious diseases.

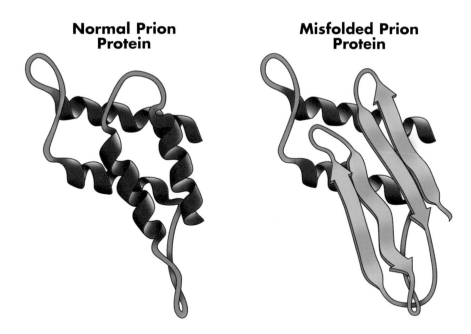

Normal Prion Protein

Misfolded Prion Protein

Scientists believe that mad cow disease and other TSEs are caused by misfolded prions, a type of protein.

transmissible spongiform encephalopathies

In 1984 a worried farmer in West Sussex, England, called in a veterinarian to look at his sick milk cow. The cow sometimes ran from the farmer in panic. Other times she charged him aggressively. The puzzled vet watched the animal as she staggered around her pen, back legs pathetically crisscrossing like a broken pair of scissors. Neither the farmer nor the vet had ever seen anything like this "mad cow" before. But she was only the first. During the next ten years, more than 200,000 cows in Great Britain and Europe developed the awful new disease, and 4.5 million cattle were destroyed in an attempt to stop its spread.

Cows that may have been exposed to BSE must be killed to prevent the disease from spreading.

Cows aren't normally carnivorous animals. But cattle farmers discovered they could use a ground-up mixture that included parts of slaughtered sheep as a cheap source of protein for their animals. Scientists believe mad cow disease first appeared in British cattle in 1984 when sheep that died from scrapie were added to cattle feed. Cows that died of mad cow disease were then ground up into meal and fed to other cows, spreading the disease.

The fact that scrapie—the prion disease found in sheep—crossed the species barrier to cattle is entirely due to human intervention. TSEs are believed to occur only in the brain and spinal cord, so it's unlikely that cattle would ever have ingested the infectious prions on their own.

Several years passed after the first mad cow was identified in 1984 before vets realized that an epidemic of a new cattle disease was under way. Researchers discovered the brains of the affected cattle were riddled with Swiss-cheeselike holes, just like the brains of sheep that died of scrapie. By then, an estimated 500,000 tons (454,000 metric tons) of infected beef had been distributed throughout Europe.

At first, health officials didn't believe the beef posed a threat to people. But in 1995, three young people in Great Britain developed CJD symptoms. They were dead within months. Dozens more cases soon followed. Autopsies showed the pattern of spongiform encephalopathy. Until then, CJD had been a very rare disease affecting about one out of a million people.

TSEs cause Swiss-cheeselike holes to form in the brain.

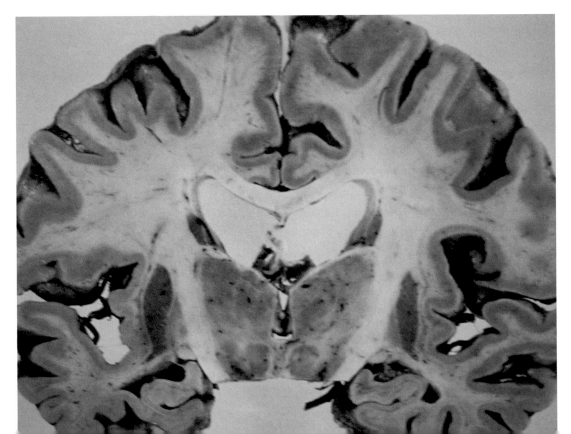

Doctors called the new human disease a variant of CJD, or vCJD. The average age at death for someone with vCJD is 28 years, compared to 68 years for CJD.

Evidence mounted that vCJD was caused by eating beef infected with mad cow disease. Zoo cats, house cats, and ferrets developed the same type of brain damage when fed TSE-infected beef. In laboratories TSE is easily transmitted between animals through contact with infected brain tissue. As the number of human victims spread across Europe, doctors discovered they had one thing in common—they had all eaten British beef in the 1980s and 1990s.

As of September 2005, 156 people in Great Britain had definite or probable vCJD. In total, about 175 people around the world, including two Americans, have developed symptoms of or died of vCJD. That doesn't seem like a lot of people. However, vCJD is always fatal, and people may not show symptoms until years after eating infected beef. Because so much infected beef was so widely distributed, no one knows how many more people will develop the disease. One British study predicts that as many as 250,000 Europeans may develop the disease over the next twenty years. Others believe the number will be far lower.

While most people get vCJD by eating infected beef, some people have gotten it after receiving organ transplants or blood transfusions from infected people. While blood banks don't yet have the technology to screen for prions, U.S. blood banks don't allow people to donate blood if they spent more than three months in Great Britain between 1980 and 1996.

A person with vCJD may first develop psychiatric symptoms such as depression and dementia (severe confusion). Then neurological signs emerge, including the inability to walk or talk.

Ultimately the brain ceases to function. Death soon follows. Certain tests may suggest that a person has vCJD, but a definite diagnosis cannot be made until the person dies and the brain is examined. We have no treatment for vCJD and no vaccine to prevent it.

Adding dead animals to cattle feed is now prohibited. However, mad cow disease still turns up in older cattle that ate infected feed before the ban. Two mad cows have been identified in the United States. One case was an animal found in Washington in 2003 that had been imported from Canada. The Washington cow was slaughtered for food even though it was so sick that it couldn't walk. Its meat was mixed with that of nineteen other cows and ended up as part of 10,000 pounds (4,536 kg) of hamburger meat. That meat was distributed in several western states before tests on the sick animal showed it had mad cow disease.

The second animal, identified in Texas in 2005, had likely eaten scrapie-infected feed before the ban. The animal from Texas did not become food for humans—it had been destined for a dog food factory. No one knows if any more Americans will develop vCJD in the next few years, but experts predict that it's likely.

CHAPTER 6

DIAGNOSING THE FUTURE:
GOOD NEWS FOR THE WORLD'S HEALTH

It is hard to grow up in some parts of the world. About 10 million children under the age of five die each year from preventable causes such as infectious disease and hunger. Just three diseases—TB, AIDS, and malaria—account for seven to eight million deaths worldwide each year. It's hard to comprehend such huge numbers. Try starting small. First, imagine that everyone in your math class died. Then suppose that everyone in your school died. How about if everyone in New York City (population 8 million) died?

Yet a tragedy of that size happens every year and goes unnoticed by most of us. Because you don't hear about malaria or yellow fever or Ebola hitting your neighborhood, it's hard to get a handle on the numbers. But each of those people who died had parents or children, sisters or brothers, and friends. Each of their lives was important to someone. And each of their lives should be important to us because we are as interconnected with the world's people as if they lived down the street from us.

We live in a global society, where a single mosquito or migrating bird carried WNV, a virus new to the Western Hemisphere, from Africa to New York City. We live in a time when a few sick airline passengers carried SARS, a virus that was entirely new to humans, from Asia to the rest of the world within days. As people continue to destroy Earth's forests and natural habitats, displaced animals, birds, and insects are likely to spread more previously unknown microbes to humans. And it won't take long for these infectious organisms to spread around the world.

human versus microbe

In the face of numerous emerging and reemerging diseases, humans have mounted a vigorous defense against these invisible invaders. Around the world, governments are speeding up research efforts, propping up once-sagging public health departments, and stockpiling antibiotics and vaccines. Activities such as studying microbial genetics, developing vaccines, and preparing for possible bioterrorism attacks are attracting talented people as well as increased funding.

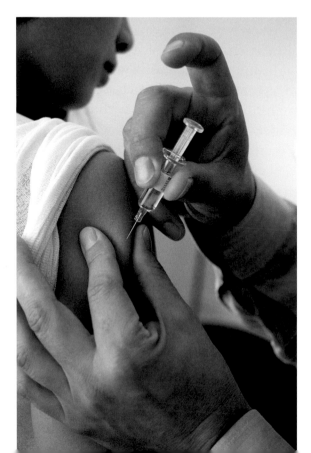

Vaccinations are an important and effective way of preventing infectious disease.

While infectious diseases will likely remain a major challenge in the foreseeable future, global health officials are quick to point out successes. Dr. Gro Harlem Brundtland, director-general of WHO, noted that the world identified SARS and stopped it dead in its tracks in one hundred days. "We've seen unprecedented international solidarity against a shared microbial threat of unknown dimensions," she said. "SARS opened the world's eyes to the magnitude of damage and disruption a new disease can cause in sectors far beyond health," she added, referring to the widespread economic impact of the outbreak.

While we have much of the knowledge and technology needed to tackle infectious diseases, there's still a long way to go. A report from the Institute of Medicine (IOM) states, "AIDS is out of control in much of sub-Saharan Africa, India, China, and elsewhere; bioterrorism has become a reality. The relentless rise of antibiotic resistance continues. We have no viable strategy for the replacement of obsolete antibiotics, and efforts to develop vaccines for malaria and HIV are disappointing."

The IOM has recommended steps that nations can take to address the ongoing threat of infectious diseases. First, we must improve global surveillance for these diseases. Many of the world's poorest countries cannot track causes of illness and death, making it difficult to identify trends in infectious diseases in those regions. In the United States, we must rebuild public health departments and clinics so that everyone can get medical care. The National Institutes of Health spends billions of dollars on research every year. This money will help us to provide quick responses to disease outbreaks, whether they occur naturally or result from bioterrorism.

GLOW GERMS

Scientists recently unveiled a new method to detect the presence of deadly pathogens. First, they added a jellyfish protein to mouse B lymphocyte cells—white blood cells that search out and destroy foreign invaders. When a virus or bacterium locks onto surface antibodies of the jellyfish-lymphocyte combo cell, the cell releases a burst of calcium and the jellyfish protein glows an eerie blue.

Next, researchers inserted DNA for antibodies to diseases such as anthrax, smallpox, and plague into the jellyfish-lymphocyte cell. When the new antibodies recognize the target pathogen, the cell releases calcium and starts glowing. It used to take several hours to identify an organism, but with the new technique, it takes only minutes.

This new biological sensor is called Cellular Analysis and Notification of Antigen Risks and Yields, or CANARY. It can also be used to identify harmful bacteria such as *E. coli O157:H7* and parasites that may contaminate our food and water. It can let doctors know right away what's making someone sick so that treatment can begin immediately.

Scientists and doctors must develop better and faster ways to accurately diagnose all infectious diseases. For example, years ago it took days for laboratories to test for HIV. But new HIV tests performed on blood or saliva in clinics and doctors' offices produce results in as few as ten minutes.

A speedy diagnosis helps ensure that the right medications can be started as soon as possible. Proper treatment is especially important when prescribing antibiotics. We need new antibiotics to replace older ones that are no longer as effective as they once were. We must also create new and better vaccines to prevent emerging and reemerging diseases such as Marburg, malaria, and TB.

Specific challenges exist for diseases carried by insects and other animals. We must find ways to reduce contact between humans and these creatures as much as possible. But we must do this without using chemicals that pollute the environment or cause suffering to people or animals. Public health officials around the world need up-to-date training in infectious diseases. Finally, countries everywhere must renew the global commitment to cooperative research.

now for the good news

While much remains to be done to protect the world against infectious diseases, there's also some good news. Scientists have sequenced (figured out) the entire human genome. The genome contains all the information the human body needs to live and grow. Differences in our genomes can lead to differences in how individuals respond to certain medications. As a result of knowing the human genome, doctors will be able to make medications safer and more effective. They will one day be able to examine a patient's DNA to determine which treatment is likely to produce the greatest benefit. The medications will be personalized to take into account the small differences in how people respond to them. Gene therapy—changing the way genes work—may eventually provide a way to bolster human immunity to all infectious diseases so that people can naturally fight off illness.

Doctors can study DNA chips (above) *to understand the way genes affect immunity as well as to identify pathogens.*

The genomes of many pathogens have also been profiled. Knowing the DNA structure of infectious organisms helps us to identify them more quickly. Soon doctors won't have to wait days to find out what's making someone sick. Instead, DNA testing will be able to identify the suspect pathogen in a hurry. Other tests look for antibodies to invading organisms in the patient's blood. One new test has the potential to identify bacteria and viruses in just minutes.

Just as bacteria invade human cells, viruses called bacteriophages invade bacterial cells. When a bacteriophage reaches a bacterium, it does what viruses always do—it injects its genetic material into the bacterium. Scientists are experimenting with modifying bacteriophages so that they deliver treatments directly to bacteria. If the bacteriophage's genetic material has been modified to include instructions for making an antibiotic-like substance, the bacterium will be killed without harm to surrounding healthy cells. Imagine viruses doing something that actually helps us for a change! Researchers believe bacteriophages will play a

Sleeping under a mosquito net reduces the risk of contracting malaria.

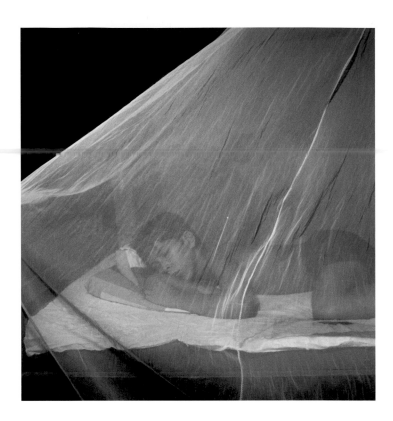

starring role in the fight against infectious diseases by becoming the antibiotics of the future.

A good part of the world's research into infectious diseases is aimed at controlling malaria. While some scientists are racing to develop a malaria vaccine, others are looking at better ways to control the mosquitoes that carry it. Small advances can make a big difference. Health officials urge the millions of people living in areas where malaria is endemic to drape insecticide-treated mosquito netting over their beds. New nets are effective for four years, compared to old nets that worked for only one year. Scientists are also experimenting with coating nets with a fungus that is harmless to people but weakens or kills mosquitoes. Sleeping under treated mosquito nets may cut the number of malaria cases in half and reduce childhood deaths by 20 percent.

Over the past few years, scientists have discovered a new fact about infectious disease: some bacteria and viruses trigger what we've called chronic diseases. Bacteria have been implicated as a cause for stomach ulcers, infertility, some forms of arthritis, and even heart disease. Viruses have been named the culprit for certain kinds of liver and cervical cancers, leukemia, and a form of mental retardation. These discoveries are opening the door for new treatments. For example, will antibiotics become standard treatment for people with heart disease? Will antiviral medications help prevent liver cancer?

Public health officials face new challenges every day. After Hurricane Katrina struck New Orleans and surrounding areas in August 2005, the health of millions of people was at risk. Evacuees crowded into large public places such as the Louisiana Superdome, where germs could easily spread from one person to the next. Residents and rescue workers had difficulty avoiding contact with contaminated floodwaters and sludge

Hurricane Katrina left much of New Orleans and other areas of the Gulf Coast under water in August 2005.

as they struggled to recover from the disaster. The U.S. Department of Heath and Human Services set up a tracking system to monitor illnesses in areas affected by the hurricane. These systems ensured that public health officials could respond quickly at the first signs of an outbreak.

The arrival of SARS demonstrated that WHO and its international partners could respond rapidly to a new infectious disease. Global cooperation on an unprecedented scale quickly brought the virus under control. According to Dr. James Hughes, director of the CDC's National Center for Infectious Diseases, "The SARS experience was a fire drill for a number of things, be it the next flu pandemic or a bioterrorist attack." We've learned a lot about emerging and reemerging infectious diseases in the past few years, and we're better prepared than ever before to battle the invisible invaders.

GLOSSARY

acquired immunodeficiency syndrome (AIDS): the illness caused by the HIV virus

aerosolize: distribute through the air

anthrax: a bacterial disease normally found in soil and animals that the CDC considers a prime candidate for use by bioterrorists

antibiotics: medications that fight bacterial infections

antibodies: proteins produced by the immune system to fight off invading organisms. Each antibody is specific to a particular bacterium or virus.

bacteria: simple microscopic organisms, many of which are harmless or even helpful to humans, but some of which cause serious disease

bioterrorism: the deliberate use of infectious pathogens against civilian or military populations

Borrelia burgdorferi: the bacterium that causes Lyme disease, transmitted to people by the bite of infected ticks

botulism: a bacterial disease that can cause paralysis and death. The bacterium that causes botulism produces the deadliest bacterial toxin known to humans.

Creutzfeldt-Jakob disease (CJD): the rare human disease caused by prions that results in spongelike holes in the brain. New variant CJD (vCJD) is believed to be transmitted through eating beef infected with mad cow disease.

deoxyribonucleic acid (DNA): the double-stranded, spiraling molecule inside every living cell that carries the genetic information for all the cell's proteins

Ebola fever: a viral disease with a high fatality rate that occurs in Africa

emerging disease: a disease that hasn't previously been found in humans or that may have occurred in humans before but went unrecognized

encephalitis: inflammation and swelling of the brain

endemic: commonly present in an area

epidemic: a disease outbreak that strikes many people in several regions at the same time

Escherichia coli (E. coli): a bacterium commonly found in the human body. *E. coli O157:H7* is a new strain that can cause serious illness and death.

gametocyte: the reproductive stage of the malaria parasite

gene: a portion of the DNA molecule that codes for one or more proteins and is the basic unit of heredity

hantavirus: a viral disease carried by rodents

hemoglobin: the iron-containing protein in red blood cells that carries oxygen through the body

hemorrhagic fevers: viruses such as Ebola, Lassa, and Marburg that can cause internal bleeding

host: the animal or plant in which a microorganism or parasite lives

human immunodeficiency virus (HIV): the virus that causes AIDS

immune system: the organs and tissues (including bone marrow, spleen, lymph nodes, and white blood cells) that protect the body from invading organisms

influenza: a viral illness that attacks the respiratory system

Lassa fever: a serious viral disease that can cause internal hemorrhaging

Lyme disease: a bacterial disease transmitted to humans by infected ticks

malaria: the disease caused by the *Plasmodium* parasite

Marburg fever: one of the most deadly viral hemorrhagic fevers

meningitis: inflammation and swelling of the thin membranes that surround the brain and spinal cord

merozoite: a stage in the malaria parasite's life cycle

methicillin-resistant *Staphylococcus aureus* (MRSA): a dangerous bacterial infection that resists many antibiotics, including methicillin

microbes: tiny organisms including bacteria, viruses, fungi, and parasites

Mycobacterium tuberculosis: the bacterium that causes tuberculosis

natural reservoir: an animal that normally harbors a pathogen without getting sick

opportunistic infections: infections that people with normal immune systems can fight off, usually found in people with AIDS or cancer or organ transplant recipients

pandemic: an outbreak of a disease that affects many people in many parts of the world at the same time

parasite: an organism that lives on or in another organism and gets its food from its host

pathogen: a microbe that makes people sick

plague: a disease caused by the bacterium *Yersinia pestis*. It occurs in three forms known as bubonic, pneumonic, and septicemic plague.

Plasmodium: the parasite that causes malaria

platelets: blood cells that help blood clot

prion: the damaged protein believed to cause mad cow disease, scrapie, and CJD

red blood cells: the cells in the blood that carry oxygen through the body

reemerging disease: a previously controlled disease that has strengthened or spread to new regions

ribonucleic acid (RNA): a molecule inside cells that transmits genetic information for protein synthesis within the cell

severe acute respiratory syndrome (SARS): a disease that causes severe respiratory problems

Shigella: a bacterium that causes the severe diarrhea and intestinal bleeding known as dysentery

smallpox: one of the deadliest viral diseases in human history. It no longer occurs naturally in people.

spongiform encephalopathy: a disease caused by prions that produces spongelike holes in the brain

sporozoite: the infectious stage of the malaria parasite

Staphylococcus aureus: a common bacterium found on the skin and in the nose and throat

toxin: a poisonous substance produced by animals, plants, or microbes

tuberculosis: a bacterial disease that primarily infects the lungs

tularemia: a highly infectious disease of rabbits, rodents, and humans

vaccine: a medication that prevents a specific infectious disease

vector: an organism that transmits a pathogen

virus: a tiny infectious particle that uses a host cell to reproduce itself

West Nile virus: a virus carried by mosquitoes that can cause encephalitis and meningitis

yellow fever: a serious viral disease carried by mosquitoes that is endemic in tropical areas of the world

SOURCE NOTES

22–23 Anthony S. Fauci, "Infectious Diseases: Considerations for the 21st Century," *Clinical Infectious Diseases,* February 23, 2001, http://www.journals.uchicago.edu/ CID/journal/issues/v32n5/ 001539/001539.web.pdf (September 9, 2005).

50 Charles Brockden Brown, "Arthur Mervyn; or, Memoirs of the Year 1793," *Blackmask Online,* 2001, http://www.blackmask.com/ books61c/mervyn.htm (September 9, 2005).

70 N. R. Grist, "Pandemic Influenza 1918," *British Medical Journal* December 22–29, 1979, 1632–1633.

72 Fauci, "Infectious Diseases."

72 H. C. Lane et al., "Bioterrorism: A Clear and Present Danger," *Nature Medicine* 2001, 1271–1273.

87 P. Schlangenhauf, "Malaria Vaccine Not Just around the Corner," *The Lancet Infectious Diseases* 2003, 394.

96 "Speech of Dr. Gro Harlem Brundtland, Director General, WHO," *World Health Organization,* June 17, 2003, http://www.who .int/csr/sars/conference/june_ 2003/materials/presentations/ brundtland/en/ (August 3, 2005).

96 Mark S. Smolinski, Margaret A. Hamburg, and Joshua Lederberg, eds., *Microbial Threats to Health: Emergence, Detection, and Response,* 2003, http://www.nap.edu/. openbook/030908864X/html/ 227.html (August 3, 2005).

102 D. Bonn, "Closing in on the Cause of SARS," *The Lancet Infectious Diseases* 2003, 268.

SELECTED BIBLIOGRAPHY

Control of Communicable Diseases Manual. 18th ed. Washington, DC: American Public Health Association, 2004.

Drexler, Madeline. *Secret Agents: The Menace of Emerging Infections.* New York: Penguin Books, 2003.

Perlin, David, and Ann Cohen. *The Complete Idiot's Guide to Dangerous Diseases and Epidemics.* Indianapolis: Alpha, 2002.

Smolinski, Mark S., Margaret A. Hamburg, and Joshua Lederberg, eds. *Microbial Threats to Health: Emergence, Detection, and Response,* 2003. http://www.nap.edu/openbook/030908864X/html/227.html (August 3, 2005).

Vanderhoof-Forschner, Karen. *Everything You Need to Know about Lyme Disease and Other Tick Borne Disorders.* New York: John Wiley, 1997.

FURTHER READING AND WEBSITES

BOOKS

Friedlander, Mark P., Jr. *Outbreak: Disease Detectives at Work.* Minneapolis: Lerner Publications Company, 2003.

Friedlander, Mark P., Jr., and Terry M. Phillips. *The Immune System: Your Body's Disease-Fighting Army.* Minneapolis: Lerner Publications Company, 1998.

Jacobs, Francine. *Breakthrough: The True Story of Penicillin.* New York: Dodd, Mead, 1985.

Murray, Polly. *The Widening Circle: A Lyme Disease Pioneer Tells Her Story.* New York: St. Martin's Press, 1996.

Preston, Richard. *The Demon in the Freezer.* New York: Random House, 2002.

Ratcliff, J. D. *Yellow Magic: The Story of Penicillin.* New York: Random House, 1945.

Storad, Conrad J. *Inside AIDS: HIV Attacks the Immune System*. Minneapolis: Lerner Publications Company, 1998.

Walters, Mark Jerome. *Six Modern Plagues and How We Are Causing Them*. Washington: Island Press/Shearwater Books, 2003.

Yancey, Diane. *Tuberculosis*. Brookfield, CT: Twenty-First Century Books, 2001.

WEBSITES

Alliance for the Prudent Use of Antibiotics
http://www.tufts.edu/med/apua/
> This site includes information for consumers, patients, doctors, and nurses about the use and misuse of antibiotics.

American Public Health Association
http://www.apha.org
> This organization works to set priorities and influence policy related to public health. The website has a news section with press releases about the APHA and its concerns.

Centers for Disease Control and Prevention
http://www.cdc.gov
> This comprehensive website has special sections on antimicrobial resistance, bioterrorism and emergency preparedness, and the National Center for Infectious Diseases. The site also contains information on chronic and infectious diseases and disorders, including details about prevention and treatment. If you are planning a visit to another country, you can check here to learn about what vaccinations you might need and how to protect your health when traveling.

Forest Pathology—Parasitic Plants
http://wiww.forestpathology.org/mistle.html
> This site has lots of information on mistletoe, including mistletoe-related folklore.

Infectious Diseases Society of America
http://www.idsociety.org
> This site has information about bioterrorism, HIV, and emerging infections, as well as material for doctors and other health-care workers.

Institute of Medicine
http://www.iom.edu
> The IOM covers many health topics including mental health, child health, food and nutrition, aging, women's health, and diseases.

Lyme Disease Foundation
http://www.lyme.org
> The Lyme Disease Foundation presents information about Lyme Disease as well as other tick-borne diseases. It explains how to reduce your chance of getting bit by ticks and what to do if you find a tick on your body.

Microbe—Stalking the Mysterious Microbe
http://www.microbe.org
> Microbiologist Sam Sleuth needs your help solving microbe mysteries! This site, run by the American Society for Microbiology, tells all about all kinds of microbes and also lists a number of experiments to try at home.

National Institute of Allergy and Infectious Diseases
http://www.niaid.nih.gov
> The website of this organization, which is part of the National Institutes of Health, covers health topics ranging from biodefense to vaccine research. The "News" section tells about recent scientific discoveries.

Tuberculosis—Stop Tuberculosis
http://www.stoptb.org
> This site covers TB around the world. It includes fact sheets about the basics of TB, the global plan to stop TB, the relationship between TB and poverty, and World TB Day.

World Health Organization
http://www.who.int/en
> The World Health Organization's website covers health topics from around the world. Click on the name of a country to find out its specific health concerns. Learn more about WHO's activities and check out "WHO sites" for information on specific diseases and conditions.

INDEX

ABOUT THE AUTHOR

Connie Goldsmith is a registered nurse with a bachelor of science degree in nursing and a master of public administration degree in health care. In addition to writing several nonfiction books for middle school and upper-grade readers, she has also published more than two hundred magazine articles, mostly on health topics for adults and children. She lives near Sacramento, California.

PHOTO ACKNOWLEDGMENTS

The images in this book are used with permission of:Center for Disease Control and Prevention Public Health Image Library (CDC), pp. 1, 20, 51, 82 (left); CDC/Courtesy of Larry Stauffer, Oregon State Public Health Laboratory, p. 2; CDC/Dr. Erskine Palmer, backgrounds on pp. 3, 19, 38–39, 49, 72–73, 97; © Christian Keenan/Getty Images, p. 8; © Sven Torfinn/Panos Pictures, p. 13; PhotoDisc Royalty Free by Getty Images, pp. 15, 68; © Scott Barrow, Inc./SuperStock, p. 17; CDC/Anthony Sanchez, p. 22; © Biomedical Imaging Unit, Southampton General Hospital/Photo Researchers, Inc., p. 24; © BSIP, SERCOMI/Photo Researchers, Inc., 28; © Todd Strand/Independent Picture Service, p. 29; © Scott Camazine/Photo Researchers, Inc., p. 32 (left); © Larry Mulvehill/Photo Researchers, Inc., p. 32 (right); © Dr. Dennis Kunkel/Visuals Unlimited, p. 37; CDC/Matthew J. Arduino, DRPH; Janice Carr, p. 39; © Dr. Fred Hossler/Visuals Unlimited, p. 42; © Reuters NewMedia Inc./CORBIS, p. 47; © Science VU/CDC/Visuals Unlimited, p. 48; Stephen Ausmus/Agricultural Research Service, USDA, p. 49 (Main); © Science VU/Visuals Unlimited, p. 54; CDC/James Gathany, p. 57; © David N. Davis/Photo Researchers, Inc., 59; Pierre Formenty/World Health Organization, p. 61; © Dr. F. A. Murphy/Visuals Unlimited, p. 62; CDC/C. Goldsmith, P. Feorino, and E.L. Palmer, p. 65; © Dr. Fred Hossler/Visuals Unlimited, p. 66; © CORBIS, p. 71; © Steve Sandford/ZUMA Press, p. 75; CDC/Photo Researchers, Inc., p. 76; CDC/Dr. Fred Murphy, p. 78; © Dr. Gopal Murti/Photo Researchers, Inc., p. 80; © London School of Hygiene/Photo Researchers, Inc., p. 82 (right); AP/Wide World Photos, p. 87; © P. Ashton/South West News Service/CORBIS SYGMA, p. 90; © Matt Polak/CORBIS SYGMA, p. 91; © La/Caretti.Bredeloup/Photo Researchers, Inc., p. 95; Mitch Doktycz, Life Sciences Division, Oak Ridge National Laboratory; U.S. Department of Energy Human Genome Program, <http://www.ornl.gov.hgmis>, p. 99; © MARK EDWARDS/ Peter Arnold, Inc., p. 100; Kyle Niemi/U.S. Coast Guard, p. 101.

Front cover: CDC/Dr. Erskine Palmer (top) and © Craig Aurness/CORBIS (bottom).